&

The State of Black
Speculative Fiction

Eugen Bacon & Milton Davis

Academia
Lunare
LUNA PRESS
PUBLISHING

First published by Luna Press Publishing, Edinburgh, 2020

"Still She Visits" first pub. in *Unsung Stories*, May 2020
"The Swarm" first pub. in *Steampunk Writers Around the World*, Vol. I, 2017.

www.lunapresspublishing.com

ISBN-13: 978-1-913387-33-4

Contents

Part One - The State of Black Speculative Fiction   v

The State of Black Speculative Fiction
Eugen Bacon & Milton Davis   1

Part Two - Hadithi   31

Still She Visits - Eugen Bacon   33

The Water's Memory - Eugen Bacon   45

Baba Klep - Eugen Bacon   56

Ancestry - Eugen Bacon   68

Carnival - Milton Davis   72

Down South - Milton Davis   112

The Swarm - Milton Davis   134

The question of what compels writers to write and then to write particular stories is one that writers, readers and critics have been asking for centuries.
(Enza Gandolfo, 2014)[1]

As a writer you take on aspects of your characters and if you are not careful the world you are creating begins to blend with the world you actually inhabit.
(Christos Tsiolkas, 2008)[2]

1. Gandolfo, Enza. 2014. Take a walk in their shoes: Empathy and emotion in the writing process. *TEXT, 18* (1). http://www.textjournal.com.au/april14/gandolfo.htm.
2. Tsiolkas, Christos. 2008. *Interview*: Interviewed by Belinda Monypenny and Jo Case. http://www.readings.com.au/interview/christos-tsiolkas.

Part One

The State of Black Speculative Fiction

The State of Black Speculative Fiction

Eugen Bacon & Milton Davis

Abstract

As speculative fiction authors are increasingly curious and experimental in a competitive publishing industry, crossing genres to subvert the reader's expectations, writers of colour are ever more claiming their right to tell their own stories in invented worlds with characters they can identify with. This new brand of writing is taking form in small press afrofuturistic dystopias, myths and epics delivered to a growing readership that is openminded and inquisitive. But, until black speculative fiction is normalised, there's still a long way to go.

Eugen Bacon

Crossing genre in speculative fiction

Speculative fiction has over decades equipped authors like Octavia Butler with the foundations to cultivate inclusive worlds and characters. (Bacon 2019b, 7)

Genre crossing is stepping out, going beyond genre (Bacon 2019b, 112). It is blending writings, subverting the reader's expectations by writing 'different' (2017, 32). It means deconstructing, breaking boundaries in modes of fiction, sometimes crossing into speculative fiction: experimental, adventurous fiction that blends genre.

Speculative fiction is creative fiction skilfully woven to comprise one or more elements of science fiction, fantasy, horror and the paranormal, and subgenres of both (2019a, 43). It allows extraordinary' storytelling in the literal sense of the word—odd, unexpected, where fiction is an immeasurable frontier and nothing is a limit (2019b, 7). If speculative fiction is about 'what if', about extrapolating, then crossing genre and subverting the reader's expectations is a promising way of giving in to speculation (36).

But speculative fiction is a genre that is somewhat regarded with suspicion by believers of traditional genre fiction as it defies adherence to strict rules of what constitutes science fiction, fantasy and horror. Such advocates would frown upon a stubborn deviant that is potentially not a 'genre' but a miscreant that bends forms of writing and refuses to be managed within rules. Yet as Orson Scott Card might have had in mind with the term 'the infinite boundary', speculative fiction is by definition 'geared towards an audience that wants strangeness—stories that contradict a known or supposed law of nature' (1990, 30).

Writing speculative fiction: critical and cultural approaches (Bacon 2019b) explores how writers such as Harlan Ellison, Margaret Atwood, Ursula Le Guin, J.R.R. Tolkien, H.G. Wells and William Golding, some of whom refuse to be labelled genre writers, integrate the literary into their speculative fiction works. Crossing speculative and literary fiction means integrating transferrable characteristics such as an interplay of poetic language, style and structure as a means of contributing to the 'quality of form' (115) in speculative fiction.

Ellison, vociferous against genre labelling, insisted that he did fiction that was more like Kafka or Poe, that he was a writer who wrote about the heart in conflict with itself (Mabe 1988). In his Promethean themed short story 'I have no mouth, and I must scream' (1967), Ellison applied literary allusion (indirect references) to an apocalyptic nightmare where a machine seeks revenge on its makers. Literary elements are dominant in this story, especially in the world building where Ellison offers colourful imagery of the chill, the oily breeze through the machine's cavern, the sloughs of despond and vales of tears … as the first-person narrator offers insights to his plight.

Like Ellison, Atwood has written literary works inspired by speculative fiction. Her story collection *Stone Mattress: Nine Wicked Tales* (2015) shows elements of the story cycle in the literary world. In the history of the story cycle, nineteenth- and twentieth-century American authors adapted and expanded the short story to relay subversive ideas without alienating the audience. In Atwood's collection, some stories are held together by thematic ties, such as repeating characters (and tales about tales) in self-sufficient narratives across the book. In a war of words with Ursula Le Guin, Atwood insists her work—including her dystopian novel *The Handmaid's Tale* (1985) that draws attention to gender, religion and power, or the apocalyptic *Oryx and Crake* (2003) that is part of the MaddAddam trilogy—is not science fiction, but is rather comfortably placed in literary speculative fiction. In her writing, Atwood bends genre and finds reward: she was named Officer, Order of Canada in

1973; was shortlisted for the Booker Prize in 1987, 1989, 1996, 2003, 2005, 2007 and won it in 2000 for her novel *The Blind Assassin* (2001). She came into resurgence with her latest offering *The Testaments* (2019) that shared the 2019 Booker Prize with Bernardine Evaristo's *Girl, Woman, Other* (2019), and won the Goodreads Choice Awards Best Fiction 2019.

Like Atwood, Ursula Le Guin, a 1975 Hugo and Nebula award winner, may be considered a literary writer. Le Guin showcased vivid prose in her dystopian novel *The Dispossessed* (1974). Her experimental, idealistic works fit within the definition of literary speculative fiction with richly invented worlds, made-up languages and imaginative presentations. There is a large presence of language and sophistication in the created world inside the fictional realm of Le Guin's Earthsea books, where knowledge of the language of magic, the language of the dragons, the language of nature, the language of creation … is power.

In encompassing hybridity in genres and subgenres that include fairy tales, dark fantasy, myths, legends, magical realism, gothic, cyberpunk, utopia, dystopia, alternate history, steampunk, horror and the paranormal, speculative fiction is globally redefining itself in cross-over fiction, even from award-winning authors such as Stephen King, Nora K. Jemisin, Octavia Butler, Ray Bradbury, William Golding, Jane Rawson, who wed genre fiction with literary fiction 'to the thrill of a broader audience who find stimulation in speculation and appreciate fluidity in language, creative vision and play' (Bacon 2019a, 50).

Placing a work in the open genre of speculative fiction

allows a reader to approach it with an open mind, to stop asking the question: Is it science fiction? Is it fantasy? (Bacon 2019b, 57). In exploring their curiosity and for an edge in a competitive industry, more and more writers are crafting speculative fiction, and more and more readers are unwittingly consuming it as they follow writers whose works bend genre (Bacon 2019a, 46).

The rise of black speculative fiction

Australian-based Lachlan Walter, in his article 'The (not so Sudden) Rise of World Science Fiction' (2019) concedes that speculative fiction is still predominantly a white, Western genre. He takes into account the works of Mary Shelley, H. G. Wells, Isaac Asimov, Arthur C. Clarke, Ray Bradbury, J. G. Ballard, Brian Aldiss, Philip K. Dick, Michael Moorcock, William Gibson, Neal Stephenson, China Miéville and Paolo Bacigalupi (34), and one finds it hard to argue against his observation.

Walter attributes this 'whiteness' to speculative fiction's evolution in the 19th century in the US and Europe, a time when the black voice was generally a silent one across all genres, not just genre fiction. In the US, in particular, even as radical abolitionism against slavery, civil war and emancipation was taking root, it was still a hazardous endeavour to raise the black voice, especially in the post-slavery south.

But things are changing.

The article 'Writing myself in' (Bacon 2019c) explores a quest for community, a push to locate affinity with the characters of one's fiction. It opens with:

'Where are the black people?' Me, at the 2019 Aurealis awards in Melbourne, an annual celebration of Australian speculative fiction. I looked about the room and it struck me just how 'white' Australia is.

And I wondered about speculative fiction—is it a 'white' genre? Yet I also wondered about the inhibited diversity in the room—was it representative of speculative fiction writers, or just of the Australian populace in that room, in Melbourne, right then? If I gallivanted across the streets of central business district, how many people of colour would I chance? (Bacon 2019c, 19)

The article goes on to recognise the author's desire to see themselves in the novels and short stories they are reading, like Nuzo Onoh's African-hued story 'Ogali' (2018). This story was published in *Aurealis*, one of Australia's largest speculative fiction magazine. 'Ogali' is an exemplar of black speculative fiction with its setting in a village and its use of the fantastical through black magic. Believable characters emerge in the once robust and cheerful teen who suffers a mysterious death; in her father who is both irate and confused; in young Amobi, portrayed as a Casanova, now horrified by the turn of fate—his wrist entrapped in the girl corpse's grip, and in the witchdoctor and his chanting, urging the petrified young man to confess his crime:

'Amobi, son of Obioha of Okoro clan, lift your shameless bottom from the floor and explain yourself to us before I curse you with the itchy pus-penis and eternal sterility, you disgraceful scoundrel.'

Tension builds with the exploration of the young

woman's death, and Amobi's possible hand in it. Tension peaks to a climax when the dead body acts on its own in supernatural ways to draw attention to its killer.

In another story, a brother-sister team of Australian Aboriginal writers Ambelin Kwaymullina and Ezekiel Kwaymullina made waves with their young adult novel book *Catching Teller Crow* (2018). The book won the 2019 Victorian Premier's Literary Awards in the Young Adult category, 2018 Aurealis Award and was nominated in a number of literary longlists and shortlists. A cross-genre work infused with prose poetry, the work is a paranormal story that reads like the everyday. It's YA literature that transcends cultural borders to bring to fore a very personal story that is also universal despite its black protagonist.

We get to see another black protagonist in a multicultural Australian story in *Inside the Dreaming* (Bacon 2020) by Newcon Press. In this origins story set in the heart of Sydney, the main protagonist is a black detective on a parallel quest to discover her roots.

New Zealand-based Nigerian author Myles Ojabo wrote *Black River: An Account of Christmas Preacher, a Slave Freed* (2018) as the creative artefact of his PhD completed at the Auckland University of Technology. He speaks about the story in 'Myles Ojabo, the slave experience, and the water goddess' (2019) and shares his desire to fill both a symbolic and literary gap in his family history with this story, longlisted in the 2020 Nommo Awards for Speculative Fiction by Africans.

In 2012, StoryTime (2020), a micro African press dedicated to publishing short fiction by emerging and established African writers, released *AfroSF: Science Fiction by African Writers* (2012). The magazine led by publisher Ivor W. Hartmann was formed in 2007 in response to a deficit of African literary magazines. Its 406-paged anthology was one of diversity and hope and featured stories such as Biram Mboob's 'The Rare Earth'—a dark tale of pilgrimage, exploitation and annihilation in the Congo, where a black messiah exists in a male-dominated world; Liam Kruger's 'Closing Time'—a cynical monologue of booze-driven time travel; Joan De La Haye's 'The Trial'—a futuristic world of human culling that targets prisoners, old people, artists and writers, poignantly told from the perspective of a fated author. A commonality that bound the anthology was an aspect of 'culture' in worlds bounding with African characters, suns and horizons. The stories embraced a bit of everything science fiction: teleporting, futuristic worlds in African landscapes, artificial intelligence, iris scanners, data mining, body irrigation, child regeneration, cyberpunk, space opera, aliens… and came along with themes that touched on matters prevalent to the African continent: war, crime, poverty, HIV… *AfroSF* was followed, to lesser popularity, by *AfroSFv2* (2015) and *AfroSFv3* (2018) , with *AfroSFv4* underway, all multicultural anthologies defiant to the tropes of Western-centric science fiction.

Digital small presses specialising in black speculative fiction are also becoming rampant, with examples in Aurelia Leo (2020) and its publication *Dominion: An Anthology of Speculative Fiction from Africa and the African Diaspora* (Knight & Donald, 2020)—with stories in the sub-genres of horror noire, Afrofuturism, sword and soul, steamfunk and dieselfunk; FIYAH Magazine of Black Speculative Fiction (2020), that accepts stories by and about black people of the

African diaspora; Farafina Books (2020); and Cosmic Roots and Eldritch Shores that published Innocent Chizaram Illo's 'Red Crows' (2019). Other publishers of speculative fiction by Africans include The Kalahari Review (2020), Omenana (2020), Sub-Saharan Magazine (2020), The Dark Magazine (2020), and more.

An 'other' like me

Octavia Butler finally decided to 'write herself in' because the stories of her time did not feature an 'other' like her. She wrote speculative fiction of change, sexism, power and politics, with black heroine protagonists as in *Fledgling* (2005), a speculative fiction novel that stars a young black vampire girl.

In *Luminescent Threads: Connections to Octavia E. Butler* (2017), an anthology that pays tribute to Butler, one author Tiara Janté spoke of her attraction to Butler's novel: 'Kindred is more than a slave story. It is a woman's story. It is a Black woman's story.'

Authors like Toni Morrison were also compelled to write something they could relate to. She stated:

My deepest passion was reading. At some point—not early, I was 35 or 36—I realised there was a book that I wanted very much to read that really hadn't been written, and so I sort of played around with it in trying to construct the kind of book I wanted to read.
Toni Morrison, Time Magazine, May 2008

African academic and writer Namwali Serpell's award

winning essay 'On Black Difficulty: Toni Morrison and the Thrill of Imperiousness' (2019) speaks to Morrison's writing—its complexity to read, to teach, for its ambiguity, disconcerting themes and sometimes abrupt yet alluring prose.

Morrison's novels like *Love* (2003), *Sula* (1998) or *Song of Solomon* (1978) hold black cultural focus. The essential aspect of her cast is their being black, their battles with or acceptances of being black (Bacon 2019b, 36). The black novel was important to Morrison because it was able to suggest conflicts and problems, not to solve them but to reflect on them (Ghansah 2015).

Exploring Dark Short Fiction #3: A Primer to Nisi Shawl (2018) opens with an extraordinary story of a woman named Fulla Fulla and her visits to the marketplace of death. The primer introduces a highly imaginative mind proficient in conjuring. Shawl's subversive text is rich with black girl empowerment and feminist ideology.

Having co-authored *Writing the Other: A Practical Approach* (2005) with Cynthia Ward, inclusive text on diverse character representation in imaginative genres, Shawl breathes her preaching. *Exploring Dark Short Fiction* is mottled with diverse protagonists and secondary characters: Hispanics in a dystopian world. White folk in post-apocalyptic female-driven narratives. If you're a person of colour, you can see your mother, your sisters, your cousins in the brown-skinned women named Dosi, Iya or Fulla Fulla in folktales set inside villages that host markets, baobab trees and characters wearing corn rows and wiry tresses.

In her article titled 'Modern Middle Ages: *Changa's*

Safari by Milton J. Davis' (2020) on tor.com's history of black science fiction, Shawl speaks to Davis' novel. Changa's Safari is an African-rooted fantasy of the 'subversive sword-and-soul genre', featuring a strong black man, Changa, and his fight against a sorcerer's demons, while exploring new trade routes and establishing trade routes. Changa is not amenable to magic, and battles immortal shamans, in a medieval multicultural story across Indian Ocean trade routes through Asia, the Middle East and Africa, and featuring a Yoruba woman named Panya, which means rat in Swahili. The Changa Safari series includes volumes two and three, and are a good advocacy of bla(c)kness in speculative fiction.

Wole Talabi is another strong advocate with his *Incomplete Solutions* (2019), a short story collection by Luna Press Publishing. The collection is a bold and playful creation with literary fragments filled with Yoruba mythology, and interrogating recurring themes of the unknown, variability, equation, relationship, sacrifice, betrayal, transposition and escapade.

There is Nick Wood, a writer with African roots—he was born and has lived in Zambia and South Africa, before moving to New Zealand, then England. His debut novel *Azanian Bridges* (2016) was shortlisted for major awards in Africa (the Nommo Award), Europe (the British Science Fiction Award) and North America (the Campbell and the Sidewise awards), and has released *Water Must Fall* (2020) by Newcon Press, that is an African story about climate change, and set in 2048, where water companies play god and determine the fate of millions.

There is Enock I. Simbaya with *Nasomi's Quest* (2020),

black speculative fiction, a sword-and-soul adventure, that transcends the vulnerability of women in patriarchal societies. It offers up a female protagonist who undergoes her own transformation arc to discover herself in a parallel quest to save the man she loves. The story hurls the reader into the oxymoron of a female antagonist, Reema, a jilted bride who—by all sensible thinking—is justified to feel wronged. But Reema's extremes stir up abundant adventure, bewilderment and marvel to drive the story in a quest narrative with Nasomi as its heroine in a literal and spiritual journey. As Reema transmutes into a potent witch obsessed with another woman's spouse, Nasomi grows from a dream-walker to a seer, then an oracle beyond herself.

Nasomi's Quest offers a robust sense of place with its cluster of huts built of bamboo, its winding streets, avenues of baobab trees, mushroom-speckled woodlands, cold valleys, knee-deep marshes and Redlands. It mirrors an African realm with its etiquette of respect to the elders; its naming of places like Nari, Kwindi and Inkanyamba; its tribes like the Somebo, Ula, Kepe and Baula; and its traditional cuisine of beans, fried plantain, goat meat stew, sweet fritters, chicken smoked over wood fire, corn brew and wheat brew. You find mages, sorcerers, priestesses and mythical creatures such as the silent and tentacled kowasa. It is a black people story told by a black person, not to alienate the 'other' but to identify with, and give voice to, the intrinsic self.

A black people hunger still rising

This craving to see the self in literature, art and performance is manifesting itself in the reception by black people of television shows like *Black Lightning* (IMDb 2018a) based on the DC comic superhero. It's the story of a school principal Jefferson Pierce leaping into action as the legendary Black Lightning after a gang threatens his family. It's the narrative of a black superhero masked as a crime fighter against the evil overtaking his city. The hunger finds satiation in movies like the blockbuster *Black Panther* (2018a) that grossed more than $100 million in its second weekend in the US, over $1 Billion worldwide within a month of release. African Americans all over the USA raved about it in interviews and newspaper articles, acclaiming it as the science fiction movie that celebrated people of colour in its themes that addressed racism, feminism, inclusion, social injustice and political correctness.

Forbes magazine claimed it the biggest success story since *Star Wars* and *Jurassic World* (Rolli 2018). The Force had awakened in Prince T'Challa of Wakanda and his personal guard of Amazonian-clad females; nothing—not a techno-dinosaur—could stop them from saving the world. It was a heralded movie where natives spoke Xhosa, the language of Mandela.

One author wrote in relation to the beauty of Black Panther, 'I could locate my blackness all over the film's narrative and cinematography' (Johnson 2019). Another stated:

> The world of Wakanda, as depicted in the film Black Panther (2018), provided an opportunity for viewers to bask in the glorious scenes, heroic drama, Black feminist power, and guile of an African world bordering on the fantastic. Starving audiences seeking Black filmic culture

eagerly settled for Wakandan fantasy—based on the filmmaker's magnificent achievement to build a fanciful and engaging vision for Black viewers and comic-book aficionados alike. (Guthrie 2019)

Such is the sense of identity that the backlash on (especially white) critics of *Black Panther* is severe on blogs, social media and news articles, as director Terry Gilliam discovered the hard way. In her essay "Black Panther' and 'Thor: Ragnarok' Are Political Parallels, But White People Only Complain About One', feminist writer Sherronda J. Brown unleashes her fury on decriers who think the movie too political. She writes:

Superhero stories are political as f***, people just get uncomfortable when they confront racism and white supremacy head-on. (2019)

The debate does not end there, and extends to the varying definitions of Afrofuturism, a term coined by American critic Mark Dery in his 1993 essay 'Black to the Future', a somewhat contentious term among certain circles because Dery is not himself a person of colour. To some, the film was a true epitome of Afrofuturism, a cultural and somewhat activist paradigm shift by intellectuals to envision Africa anew through imagination and aspiration, awakening her traditions, combining them with magic, technology and the speculative, to empower a new rise of the continent and her people, untarnished (or redefined) by colonialism. Afrofuturism is expansive in reach, spanning literature, music, visual art, philosophy, even architecture in an awakening of the black consciousness away from slavery or colonialism to universal probabilities that are also empowering (Brooks et al. 2019). In February 2020, New York Daily News described singer Nona Hendryx's appearance as bringing Afrofuturism performance to the Metropolitan Museum of Art in a concert that would 'collapse time; past, present and future, space and place, inner and outer worlds, travelling via music and the mind to stars, quasars, suns, moons and delving into black holes' (Daniels 2020). Yet others contentiously try to contain the term 'Afrofuturism' to the African American vision and insist on 'Africanfuturism' for the non-American visions of the future by people of the African diaspora.

Provocative or not, there continues to be an emergence of groups such as the African Speculative Fiction Society (ASFS 2020), whose membership includes writers, editors, comic and graphic artists and filmmakers in the fields of speculative fiction such as fantasy, science fiction and horror, and whose stories draw on tradition, philosophy and science. The ASFS administers the Nommo awards that are 'an African SF prize for Africans by Africans that honours our stories and how we choose to tell them'—according to the website. The organisation's inclusive definition of who is African includes citizens of African countries, people born on the continent and raised there for substantial periods of time, citizens or people born on the continent who live abroad, people who have at least one African parent or Africans without papers, and some migrants to African countries.

There is the State of Black Science Fiction (2020), that is an online community of black writers and artists, and the African Science Fiction and Fantasy Reading Group (2020) on Facebook, where writers have conversations about stories, publications, awards and challenges. The existence of these groups, and others of a similar nature, attracting creatives who are people of colour, suggests a hunger for black people stories, but who will write them?

Australia, for example, is plagued by her own shameful past in dealing with indigenous people—systematic killings and cultural purgings, stolen generations and forbiddance of dialects now nearly extinct. Now part of the 'sorry' invites protocols (Australian Council for the Arts, 2007) on who can write what story. That black people should tell their own story... but what kind of story do they wish to tell? And where does speculative fiction fit in these, bearing in mind the explicable hesitancy of non-black people to write black speculative fiction.

This means stories like Nuzo Onoh's 'Ogali' and the Kwaymullina's *Catching Teller Crow* are simply baby steps, not nearly enough in the recognition of speculative fiction by black people. The US is ahead, as more and more authors of colour continue to write themselves in. Authors like Milton Davis (2020) and his tales of sisters of the spear; bounty hunters in the quest of a valuable book from here to Timbuktu; priestesses in leopard clans; rising phoenixes in flitting shadows and full moons; otherworldly creatures, demons and immortals in mysterious realms, and the black fantastic.

The state of black speculative fiction in the US and the rest of the world—Milton Davis

Award winning author and small press publisher, Milton Davis, shares his first-hand experience:

The growth of black speculative fiction in the US and other parts of the world found its energy in the hands of independent black writers. Like me, many black science fiction and fantasy readers were disappointed with the dearth of books that featured characters that not only looked like us but dealt with experiences, traditions and cultures we were intimately familiar with.

In the tradition of renowned authors Toni Morrison and Octavia Butler, these black writers decided to write stories they could identify with themselves. The difference was that this was the time of the internet and print on demand, two technological advances that enabled the emergence and growth of the independent black speculative fiction movement in the US.

Print on demand gave independent authors a cost-effective means to produce books while social media gave them the platform to share their books with like-minded readers, and develop platforms to support their fans and followers.

My interest in science fiction and fantasy was ignited by a college English professor who was impressed by my writing and thought I should be an English major. She used science fiction and fantasy to get me interested, and it almost worked. Although it did motivate me to write, it didn't persuade me to change my major.

My love for black speculative fiction evolved soon after I published my first book *Meji* (2010). *Meji* is a celebration of African history and culture written as an epic fantasy. It was at this same time that I was introduced into the culture of black speculative fiction. That's when my attraction to this interpretation of black speculative fiction began.

Up to that point I didn't know enough authors nor was I aware of enough books for this type of fiction to matter. But like me, I discovered many writers that were tired of waiting for stories that reflected them physically and culturally and began writing their own stories.

Though many of us felt isolated in our endeavours, we soon realised we were not alone. We found each other through social media, and it was refreshing to know that there were others creating a different narrative for science fiction and fantasy, a narrative that put us front and centre.

My first encounter with such writers was with the Black Science Fiction Society. Many of the writers I met on this site are still fellow cohorts to this day, with many of them going on to publish with mainstream publishing companies. Authors such as Nuzo Onoh, Namwali Serpell, Wole Talabi, Suyi Davies Okungbowa, Tade Thompson, Nick Wood, Balogun Ojetade, Carolle McDonnell, Ronald Jones, Valjeanne Jeffers, Letitia Carelock, Alan Jones, Marcus Haynes, Jessica Hosten, Nicole Smith, Cerece Renee Murphy and others have built significant followings and helped to carve a niche that continues to influence mainstream publishers and authors. In 2020, Nigerian science fiction, fantasy and horror writer Suyi Davies Okungbowa signed a book deal with Orbit for a three-book fantasy series, The Nameless Republic, whose speculative world is inspired by West African empires (2020).

Through social networking the word spread of new writers coming together to produce black speculative fiction. After a successful blog tour spearheaded by author Alicia McCalla, we decided to take our movement offline with the creation of The State of Black Science Fiction forum. The purpose of the forum was to create a platform to discuss black speculative fiction, where it was at the present time and where it was headed. The forum was first held at the Georgia Institute of Technology. To support the forum, we formed a Facebook group with the same title, The State of Black Science Fiction (2020). The forum has been held in various venues over the years, however, it's the Facebook group that has become the biggest success.

The State of Black Science Fiction group has become a gathering point for creators and consumers of African/ African Diaspora-based speculative fiction, boasting over seventeen thousand members across the world.

The effect of indie black speculative fiction has been significant. Before its growth, there were unwritten restrictions applied to African/African Diaspora writers attempting to publish in the genres. The concept of 'gatekeepers' was, and still is, real. A common question posed to black creators when submitting stories was: 'Does the character have to be black?' This question came from the supposed belief that science fiction and fantasy was a white-, male-dominated genre and its readers would not be interested in stories that focused on characters that didn't reflect them.

Anthologies have been very important in the spread of black speculative fiction. Just like *Dark Matter: A Century of Speculative Fiction from the African Diaspora* (2000), edited by Sheree Renee Thomas, anthologies have played an important part in the growth of independent Black Speculative Fiction. My first anthology, *Griots: A Sword and Soul Anthology* (2011), was created to give black indie writers the opportunity to express themselves in the genre of word and Sorcery. Before *Griots*, the only black writer to consistently publish sword and sorcery was Charles R. Saunders, creator of the Imaro stories and the subgenre of sword and soul. We co-edited *Griots* and the follow up anthology, *Griots: Sisters of the Spear* (2014).

Under MVmedia, I continued to use anthologies to break the barriers set up by major publishing gatekeepers. Most notably were *Steamfunk!* (2013), an Afro-centric steampunk anthology, *The City, A Cyberfunk Anthology* (2015) and the Dark Universe series, a space opera collection with stories by various black science fiction writers, centred in an Afrocentric galactic empire. Other anthologies, such as *Sycorax's Daughter* (2017), edited by Kinitra Brooks PhD, Linda D. Addison and Susana Morris PhD (Editor), exposed the reading public to a plethora of black women authors that excel in the horror genre.

When I began publishing, I was often asked why I thought it was important to write speculative fiction stories from an African/African Diaspora perspective. The answer was simple: I write for a black audience. As a reader, I missed seeing a story told from my perspective. I longed for stories that depicted a protagonist who looked like me. I was negatively impacted by stories that showed black characters in stereotypical roles.

Other authors that pursued the same path did so for

similar reasons. However, we all knew that good writing transcends demographics, and that has been the case with our works to date.

The vast number of black speculative fiction books by independent authors have had a positive effect on genre literature. I have sold over 10,000 books in my ten years of publishing. Combined with my fellow writers it wouldn't be far off to estimate the number of books sold or produced by independent black authors to over a hundred thousand.

This volume of books has changed the expectations of readers. Instead of waiting years for the release of speculative fiction by a writer of African descent, such books are published on a daily basis, in accessible media, allowing readers to invest into this unique perspective.

A question was raised at our recent State of Black Science Fiction panel discussion; has black speculative fiction arrived? The answer was encouraging yet cautious. Although all panellists agreed that much progress has been made, the consensus was that—until black speculative fiction is normalised—there's much work to be done.

Conclusion

There's a growth of black speculative fiction that has found energy in the hands of independent black writers and small presses, each increasingly bending genre to subvert the readers' expectations, and tell black people stories in invented worlds with heroes and heroines that people of colour can identify with. This new brand of writing is taking the form of cross-genre afrofuturistic dystopias, myths and epics to a growing readership that is openminded and inquisitive. But, until more readers, publishers, agents and literary award judges start to pay more notice, until black speculative fiction becomes normalised, we still have a long way to go.

References

African Speculative Fiction Society (ASFS). 2020. Accessed 2 March 2020. <http://www.africansfs.com/about>

African Science Fiction and Fantasy Reading Group. 2020. Accessed 2 March 2020. <https://www.facebook.com/groups/african.fantasy>

Atwood, Margaret. 2019. *The Testaments*. New York: Nan. A. Talese.
---2015. *Stone mattress: Nine wicked tales*. London: Virago Press.
---. 2003. *Oryx and Crake* (MaddAddam #1). Toronto: McClelland and Stewart.
---. 2001. *The blind assassin*. New York: First Anchor Books.

Aurelia Leo. 2020. Accessed 23 December 2019. <https://aurelialeo.com>

Australian Council for the Arts. 2007. *Protocols for producing Indigenous Australian writing*. Surry Hills: Australia Council.

Bacon, Eugen. 2020. *Inside the Dreaming*. Cambridgeshire: Newcon Press.
---. 2019a. 'Writing and Reading Speculative Fiction'. *Aurealis* #120 (May 2019): 43-49.
---. 2019b. *Writing Speculative Fiction*. London: Red Globe Press.
---. 2019c. 'Writing Myself In'. *Victorian Writer* (Aug/Sep 2019): 19-21.
---. 2018. 'What is AfroSF'. *Aurealis* #111 (June 2018): 41-47.
---. 2017. 'Crossing Genre: Exemplars of Literary Speculative Fiction'. *Aurealis* #105 (October 2017): 32-36.

Brooks, Kinitra, Addison, Linda D. & Morris, Susana. 2017. *Sycorax's Daughters*. California: Cedar Grove Publishing.

Brooks, Lonny, Anderson, Reynaldo, Taylor, Douglas & Baham, Nicholas. 2019. 'Introduction to the Special Issue When is Wakanda: Afrofuturism and Dark Speculative Futurity'. *Journal of Future Studies*: 24 (2). Accessed 25 December 2019. <https://jfsdigital.org/wp-content/uploads/2019/12/00-Introduction.pdf>

Brown, Sherronda, J. 2019. "Black Panther' and 'Thor: Ragnarok' Are Political Parallels, But White People Only Complain About One'. Accessed 25 December 2019. <https://wearyourvoicemag.com/entertainment-culture/black-panther-thor-ragnarok-political-parallels>

Card, Orson, Scott. 1990. *How to Write Science Fiction and Fantasy*. Ohio: Writer's Digest Books.

Daniels, Karu F. 2020. 'Nona Hendryx to bring Afrofuturism performance to Metropolitan Museum of Art with special Sun Ra tribute'. Accessed 1 March 2020. <https://www.nydailynews.com/snyde/ny-nona-hendryx-sun-ra-tribute-afrofuturism-metropolitan-museum-harlem-20200227-exv6yqunerbwpctweaukwl2iem-story.html>

Davis, Milton. 2020. Accessed 2 March 2020. <https://www.miltonjdavis.com>
---. 2015. *The City: A Cyberfunk Anthology*. Atlanta: MVmedia, LLC.
---. 2010. *Meji*. Atlanta: MVmedia, LLC.
---. *Steamfunk!* Atlanta: MVmedia, LLC.
---. (eds) 2014. *Griots: Sisters of the Spear*. Atlanta: MVmedia, LLC.
---. (eds) 2011. *Griots: A Sword and Soul Anthology*. Atlanta: MVmedia, LLC.

Ellison, Harlan. 1967. 'I Have No Mouth and I Must Scream', *If: Worlds of Science Fiction*, 17: 3, 467–483 (eBook).

Evaristo, Bernardine. 2019. *Girl, Woman, Other*. London: Hamish Hamilton.

Farafina Books. 2020. Accessed 2 March 2020. <https://farafinabooks.wordpress.com>

FIYAH Magazine of Black Speculative Fiction. 2020. Accessed 2 March 2020. <https://www.fiyahlitmag.com>

Ghansah, Rachel. Kaadzi. 2015. 'The Radical Vision of Toni Morrison'. Accessed 6 November 2019. <http://www.nytimes.com/2015/04/12/magazine/the-radical-vision-oftoni-morrison.html?_r=0>

Guthrie, Ricardo. 2019. 'Redefining the Colonial: An Afrofuturist Analysis of Wakanda and Speculative Fiction'. Journal of Future Studies: 24 (2). Accessed 25 December 2019. <https://jfsdigital.org/wp-content/uploads/2019/12/02-Guthrie-Redefining-Colonial.pdf>

Hartmann, Ivor W. 2018. *AfroSF3*. Harare: StoryTime.
---. 2015. *AfroSF2*. Harare: StoryTime.
---. 2013. *AfroSF: Science Fiction by African Writers*. Harare: StoryTime.

Illo, Innocent, Chizaram. 2019. 'Red Crows'. Accessed 23 December 2019. <https://cosmicrootsandeldritchshores.com/fiction-all/eldritch/red-crows>

IMDb. 2018a. Black Lightning. Accessed 7 November 2019. <https://www.imdb.com/title/tt6045840>
---. 2018b. Black Panther. Accessed 7 November 2019. <https://www.imdb.com/title/tt1825683>

Johnson, Amber. 2019. 'Exploring the Dark Matter(S) of Wakanda: A Quest for Radical Queer Inclusion Beyond Capitalism'.

Journal of Future Studies: 24 (2). Accessed 25 December 2019. <https://jfsdigital.org/wp-content/uploads/2019/12/01-Johnson-Exploring-the-Dark-Matter.pdf>

Knight, Zelda & Donald, Ekpeki Oghenechovwe. 2020. *Dominion: An Anthology of Speculative Fiction from Africa and the African Diaspora*. Aurelia Leo. Accessed 23 December 2019. <https://aurelialeo.com>

Kwaymullina, Ambelin & Ezekiel.2018. *Catching Teller Crow*. Melbourne: Allen & Unwin.

Le Guin, Ursula K. 1994. *The dispossessed*. New York: Harper Voyager.

Lovell, Bronwyn, 2019, 'Writing in a genre where 'nothing is out of bounds': Speculative Fiction as a transformative force'. TEXT 23(2). Accessed 6 November 2019. <https://www.textjournal.com.au/oct19/lovell_rev.htm>

Mabe, Chauncey. 1988. 'Harlan Ellison: Don't Call Me a 'Sci-fi Writer'. Accessed 6 November 2019. <http://articles.sun-sentinel.com/1988-03-13/features/8801160511_1_fiction-harlan-ellison-american-science>

Morrison, Toni. 2018. '10 Questions for Toni Morrison'. Accessed 6 November 2019. <http://content.time.com/time/magazine/article/0,9171,1738507,00.html>
---. 2003. Love. London: Chatto & Windus.
---. 1998. Sula. London: Vintage.
---. 1978. Song of Solomon. London: Vintage.

Okungbowa, Suyi Davis. 2020. 'Acquisition Announcement:

The Nameless Republic by Suyi Davies Okungbowa'. Accessed 6 February 2020. <https://www.orbitbooks.net/2020/01/16/acquisition-announcement-the-nameless-republic-by-suyi-davies-okungbowa>

Ojabo, Myles. 2019. 'Myles Ojabo, the slave experience, and the water goddess'. Accessed 24 December 2019. <https://clarerhoden.com/2019/11/15/myles-ojabo-the-slave-experience-and-the-water-goddess>
---. 2018. *Black River: An Account of Christmas Preacher, a Slave Freed.* Auckland: Dafel Books.

Omenana. 2020. Accessed 6 February 2020. <https://omenana.com>

Onoh, Nuzo. 'Ogali', *Aurealis* #118 (March 2018): xy-zz.

Pierce, Alexandra & Mondal, Mimi. 2017. *Luminescent threads: Connections to Octavia E. Butler.* Western Australia: Twelfth Planet Press.

Rolli, Bryan. 2018. 'Why 'Black Panther' is a bigger box office success story than 'Star Wars' and 'Jurassic World'. Accessed 6 November 2019. <https://www.forbes.com/sites/bryanrolli/2018/02/24/black-panther-box-office-star-wars-jurassic-world/#32b5d0244e4a>

Serpell, Namwali. 2019. 'On Black Difficulty: Toni Morrison and the Thrill of Imperiousness'. Accessed 6 February 2020. <https://slate.com/culture/2019/03/toni-morrison-difficulty-black-women.html>

Shawl, Nisi. 2020. Modern Middle Ages: Changa's Safari by Milton J. Davis. Accessed 26 February 2020. <https://www.tor.com/2020/02/25/modern-middle-ages-changas-safari-by-milton-j-davis>

---. 2018. *Exploring Dark Short Fiction #3: A Primer to Nisi Shawl*. Eric J. Guignard (ed). Los Angeles: Dark Moon Books.

Shawl, Nisi & Ward, Cynthia. 2005. *Writing the other*. Seattle: Aqueduct Press.

Simbaya, Enock I. 2020. *Nasomi's Quest*. Atlanta: Mvmedia LLC StoryTime. 2019. Accessed 4 December 2019. <https://storytime-african-publisher.blogspot.com>

Sub-Saharan Magazine. 2020. Accessed 6 February 2020. <https://subsaharanmagazine.com>

Talabi, Wole. 2019. *Incomplete Solutions*. Edinburgh: Luna Press Publishing.

The Dark Magazine. 2020. Accessed 6 February 2020. <http://thedarkmagazine.com>

The Kalahari Review. 2020. Accessed 6 February 2020. <https://kalaharireview.com>

The State of Black Science Fiction. 2019. Accessed 7 November 2019. <https://www.facebook.com/groups/blackscifi>

Thomas, Sheree Renée (ed). 2000. *Dark Matter: A Century of Speculative Fiction from the African Diaspora*. New York: Aspect - Warner Books

Walter, Lachlan. 2019. 'The (not so Sudden) Rise of World Science Fiction. *Aurealis* #125 (October 2019): 34-39.

Wood, Nick. 2020. *Water Must Fall*. Cambridgeshire: Newcon Press.
---. 2016. *Azanian Bridges*. Cambridgeshire: Newcon Press.

Part Two

Hadithi

Still She Visits

Eugen Bacon

YOU REMEMBER when you were eleven or twelve, hands fumbling with a folded cloth. The tingle of a sore nipple, the claws of muscle cramp. Each pang in your pelvis was a sword that hacked away your childhood.

Your mother waltzed into your grave-sized room. It was tiny enough to hold two coffins and a row of ghost feet. It always felt haunted. Mamm brought in her rage and suspicion in a growl that said, 'What mischief are you plotting?' even though the words were different: 'Tidy your room yet?' Furrows on her forehead, her no-nonsense gait… all now just a memory in fragments.

It was your little sister Mokgosi—her name means a call for help—who used her body to shield your secret from your mamm. Why it had to be a secret, you don't know, maybe it was to stop your mother from fraying your ears with threats about boys. How they took everything you gave, then broke you even though you were empty. How they sauntered whistling to a forever place, leaving you with mouths to feed, tiny mouths that couldn't tolerate hunger.

'Loosen, Mamm. Just ease.' Mokgosi's calming words

stood in front of your stained pad and your mother, ever grouchy like a buffalo.

Mamm looked harder at your sister and your blocked self, still with rage and suspicion, but she left the room without a word, and that didn't happen all that often. You looked at Mokgosi. She looked at you. She gave you a clean pad and soaked your blood in salted cold water, washed the nasty cloth with her bare hands, because money, money, money. There was no money to take to a shop and buy tampons.

It was then that you understood your sibling bond, even though before that you were street dogs—the way you fought. This new love moved you through bad things, like when your mother left, not just your room, but this time for good.

It's an undying love that makes you see through the hollow in Mokgosi's eyes full of dusk, so you can unsee the guts like strings falling out of her mouth, her ears. Her silent aura telling you like a movie that she's dead, please be honest.

'Sorry, I…' You clang pots, bang doors in your apartment in East Melbourne. *Thump-thwack-clang-bang.* How can you be honest to such loss?

But still Mokgosi visits.

*

Segomotsi—your name means a comfort in Setswana. Few people here know you by that name; they call you Seggie Slacken—the Aussie you married.

It's years since you travelled home. Botswana will be a stranger, the village of Lejwana even more. But with your parents gone, and without your sister Mokgosi, what's left to call home?

A girl waits opposite you at the shrink's office. She flicks through pages of a brand-new issue of *Women's Interest*. She's chewing gum. Flick, chew. The receptionist ignores you both.

You consider the receptionist, her face sharp as a pin, her nose and ponytail equally harsh. Back home, you would chat to strangers like old friends; ask about their cows, their goats, their children. Here, folk don't do that.

The psychiatrist who retrieves you has dimples. Her pensive face is complete with lines: forehead lines, crow's feet at the sidelines, marionette lines run straight upwards from the corners of her mouth. Her room is pristine, bland colours unable to touch your moods. Her leather couch is familiar, wears an easy look like the coin-slotted massage sofa at the Jam Factory in South Yarra.

You ignore Mokgosi, her hollow eyes, oozing entrails, sitting in the corner of the room. The settee in which you recline, face up to the bland ceiling, smells synthetic. Nothing like the dusky cowhide on Uncle Kopano's chairs in Lejwana, unbleached skin and hair that smells of wet mud. This leather is coffee coloured, café latte.

'How are you?' Dr Bland. Her voice matches the insipid room.

'How is she in this room?' you say.

'How is who in the room?'

'There. Can't you see?'

'What would you like me to see?'

'She looks like death but smells fresh and sweet like gazania.'

Silence.

'She was like that in life, you know. Bright yellow, hot orange, cheery purple, her temperament, sometimes the clothes she got from *mtumba*—second hand. Face of the sun, unfussy, everything she wore just fit right.'

Silence.

'Dainty, but she was the stronger of us two. With a mother like ours who had to fight for everything she got, so much that she mistook her children for combat, you needed a Mokgosi standing with a water bottle and a towel in your corner. So here she is, fully here, to fight my demons—only now she's one too. All wretched to look at, but there's strength in her scent. Sweet mango. Sometimes durian.'

*

You leap into the swimming pool at the aquatic centre. Mokgosi dangles her feet in the water, makes you touch them each turn at the wall before you somersault. It feels like a call for help, but whose—yours or Mokgosi's?

*

A week.

'Is Mokgosi in the room with us today?' asks Dr Bland.

'Right there. Same corner.'

Mokgosi who always stood by your side, but you're the one who got away. It was curiosity for the world and a scholarship that put you on a plane, and away, away, you flew.

'What's she looking at?' asks Dr Bland.

'You.'

'What's she thinking, do you know?'

'I guess—why you? She was always there for me.'

'And how do you feel right now?' asks Dr Bland.

'Cross,' you say.

'Cross—because your sister is looking at me?'

'Because work sucks. Been thinking to leave.'

Silence.

'Employee assistance programme, bereavement leave on tap, cards, flowers …' you say.

'I'm glad you took EAP—that's why you're here,' says Dr Bland.

'How can a plant so rugged be so beautiful? It grows in extreme heat, tolerates any drought, climbs out of the hardest earth to splay in vibrant colours…' You choke.

Dr Bland hands you a tissue.

*

A week.

'Surprised?' Dr Bland. Sometimes she's like this, prods you with a question. 'Why so? You say Mokgosi surprised you?'

'When Mamm left… her leaving was not the kind of walkaway our father did: *Grabbing cigarettes, be right back.* A beast in the wind swallowed him whole, no one saw him again. No, Mamm's leaving was the kind that happens where shadows reach into sleep and take away a loved one.' All that fighting the world finally it took its toll. 'She ate dinner one night, rested her head on a pillow, closed her eyes and never woke up.'

'So how has your sister surprised you?'

'Mokgosi doesn't hurt like when Mamm died.'

Mokgosi slips from her corner, her gazania bloom smell

tightly closed—today she's odourless. She shuffles to the
settee in which you recline. Traces with her gnarled finger a
tear that brooks its way round your nose to the edge of your
lips.

'If Mokgosi doesn't hurt,' says Dr Bland, 'then why are
you crying?'

*

A week.

'Do you know that the gazania flower doesn't bloom on a dark
or stormy night?'

'Is that how you feel today?' Dr Bland. 'Dark and stormy?'

'I feel far.'

'What do you mean?'

'Too far to mourn.'

'Why didn't you go to Botswana when she was sick?'

'Work, stuff.'

'How are you dealing with being far now?'

'I sent money. World Remit. To help with the funeral.'

Silence.

'But they didn't need it. Took them a week, a whole week
for Uncle Kopano to collect it. The chief is a friend of my
family. He paid for everything: hospital bill, ivory-finish coffin.
They didn't need my money.'

'How does that make you feel?'

Mokgosi's hollow eyes full of dusk pouring into your soul.
'What do you expect?'

Silence.

'No Tobin Brothers Funeral services in Lejwana, you know. Nobody to wash her. Nobody saying to you: *How would you like to make your coffin look? Or: We'll send out the funeral notice to your friends.* It's the women who washed her, dressed her. Put lipstick on her face. Put eye shadow, angel face. Put her in a white dress with a shiny coat. No curls in her hair; they put on a head-dress.'

Silence.

'There were drums, huge drums, Uncle said. *Doomba-doo! Doomba-doo! Doodoomba-doo! Doo! Doo! Doodoodoo!* The whole village was together, they farewelled her like a queen.'

Mokgosi in her corner, smiles at the memory.

'All of Lejwana at her doorstep. They sang, they danced, they drank. They feasted: platters of meat and rice. Chief Dikeledi paid for it. People ate fit to burst.'

Silence.

'I feel rubbish.'

Mokgosi is on the settee—how did she get there so quick? She's cradled to your breast. Her aura is red with splashes of hot pink. Her scent, dear gods, her scent. An overwhelming sweetness that reminds you of a wedding.

'What do you regret the most?' says Dr Bland.

'Being seven thousand miles from Mokgosi's grave. Far, far from home…'

Mokgosi strokes your cheeks through the sadness. 'I didn't even keep the Aussie.' Your smile is cynical. 'Slacken. The divorce was a slap in the face for him, fourth year of our marriage. No wonder he went mean after that, the slap still ringing.'

*

A week.

Today Mokgosi looks like your mother, the rage, the suspicion, black fog swirling from her empty eyes. Furrows on her head, a no-nonsense gait.

'How are you today?' Dr Bland. She sits in a comfortable silence, palms flat, parallel on her thighs. Sometimes she sprawls her arms casually on each armrest.

'Angry. ANGRY.'

'Talk to it,' says Dr Bland. 'Talk to your anger.'

Acha! Stop! Mokgosi is shaking her head, making a gargling noise. She's rocking in a corner, back against the wall like Mamm did in the kitchenette when your father evaporated.

'Why don't they call it what it is? What it is IT IS!'

'Why don't they call what?' asks Dr Bland.

'What it is IT IS she died of.'

'What do you want to call it?'

Mokgosi leaps. Her scream is full of echoes, her arms outstretched to muffle or strangle you. Entrails like tongues rush from the yawn of her gobbling mouth.

'Break the circle of silence. It's not malaria. It's not pneumonia. It's not tuberculosis.' Hands on your throat, you can't breathe, breathe. But the words fall out of your mouth: 'It's AIDS. AIDS. AIDS!'

Mokgozi's fading cry, *Arrggggh…* Then she puffs out, leaves behind a sickly sweet smell of formaldehyde.

Your wet face against Dr Bland's breast.

*

A week.

'No more Mokgosi in the room?' asks Dr Bland.

You shake your head. 'No more.'

You're surprised that something is changed in Dr Bland, in how she speaks now. She talks different. A slant in her vowels, a trail as if they're cursive with consonants. There's colour in Dr Bland. Texture.

'What do you want to talk about today?' asks Dr Bland.

'Like what?'

'Tell me anything.' Each vowel has its sound, like a sixth sense.

'I made hard decisions, the ones that made me stay. It wasn't the lightness of bills—he was more expensive to keep than me alone. I married an Aussie, but it wasn't for the fondness in his touch. Kissing him was like smooching carrion, the sex as impersonal as a bus driver's glance at dismounting passengers. I don't know why I stayed. All night as he snored, I heard sirens. *Do you have a moment?* they sang. *Tell us your name.*'

'And what's your name?' Cursive words, the tongue lingers.

You're not sure whether it's you or Dr Bland who has changed.

'My name is Segomotsi—it means a comfort in Setswana.'

*

You lie in bed, unable to sleep. You remember the hurt you forgot. The day Mokgosi died, your sense of loss was so keen, it pierced holes into your gut, and cannonballs entered those holes. You flick on the lights, look at the white of the ceiling speckled with the cream of the apartment sprinkler, a fire safety gadget with circular ridges, indents and protrusions. Three silver hooks fasten the clear of the translucent plate covering the bulb.

Had to happen in March?

Death is easier in November—New Year around the corner. Come January, you set your mind to new thinking. You leave death with the year gone. Sucks in March; you have to live with death the whole year.

*

You look at your phone: 6am.

It's Saturday.

Aquatic centre, you prefer the outdoor pool. You swim like the physio instructed: 'When you turn to breathe, level your cheek with the water surface, not nose up.' You agree with the physio: this way is less strain on your neck.

Every day is winning and losing. Sometimes more win than loss, a little more now. She still visits, Mokgosi. Unfolding in bright colours of the gazania. She's an African daisy and, like all daisies, she's complete in herself. Gazanias, like tall grasses, just more radiant, appear anywhere. There she is luminescent in the water, shimmering with the waves as you swim. Hers is a big kiss, florets and golds spreading with each stroke. Now I'm a bigger bloom, she says. Her voice buzzes rich with low notes. You should see, she says in her resonant bassoon. It's a starburst here.

You swim, swim. Sweet mango and durian: her scent in the waves.

Water enters your nose, your mouth, just enough not to unsettle. Breathing cheek level with the water, you like it. It is almost like a water hug. The sun is playful. She patterns the base of the pool with her rays. A white ray bounces off a window to reflect on your tinted goggles as you breathe. Your face is in the water. The sun's rays are a comfort, like your name. The sun feels intimate.

Like Mokgosi's gaze.

*

A week.

Silence.
    Silence.
    'Tell me anything.' Dr Bland.
    'Anything.'
    She smiles.
    Silence.
    Silence.
    'I know to see when I'm drowning,' you say.
    'Good. Make sure you keep swimming.'
    You smile.
    Silence.
    Silence.

Story within a story

I was in Melbourne, Australia, when my elder sister Flora died of AIDS in Tanzania. Amid tearing my hair in lone anguish, I crawled to a computer and started typing out a self-reflective cathartic narrative that drew from my own personal feeling of discontinuity and an awareness of being between worlds as an African Australian migrant. Later, as I focused on the self-knowledge that emerged from the act of writing the short fiction in the wake of grief, it surprised me that my primary emotion was rage. In mirroring into the creative fiction aspects of my own loss, I understood that my relationship with Segomotsi was symbiotic. I needed her as much as she needed me. As I developed her character and transferred to her my direct experiences, she responded. Without answering all my questions, Segomotsi came along with new meaning that helped me understand and process my grief.

The Water's Memory
Eugen Bacon

THE RED LEOPARD showed on the night of your wedding, when the sun, earth and moon were imperfectly aligned. You moved from the women's mirth, belly-deep and wholesome, undrowned by the sound of village drums. *Pom! Pom! Pom pi pom pi!*

Our son has found a maiden! began a chorus.

A nymphette from the lake.

The begetter of our offspring!

Pom! Pi! Po pom pi! Drums vibrated in a booming cantata as bare torsos gyrated, gleamed with animal fat.

Pure from the water nymph, sang the villagers.

Such wonder she shines.

A swish of skirts here, a sway of neck there. And the feet! Caked with dust, toes tapped their dance in sync to the drums. A spray of soil from the ground formed a cloud that lifted to the horizon where a yellow moon crossed the earth's shadow.

Fresh like the smell of rain!

Pure like a newborn,

Younger than morning dew.

Your arms glimmered with cowry shell trinkets—red,

green and yellow. Dancers pranced to fever pitch, swayed heads hugged tight with feathers. You admired your cousin Achieng, a young, free spirit with the biggest sway, her neck of an ostrich, her eyes of a gazelle.

You sat under a stringy bark tree with the rest of the young women, all virgins gleaming with animal fat rubbed on their skins. You sat next to the children. A handful of babies first perked to *pom! pi! pom!* then surrendered to sleep. Mosquitos, mellowed with drunken blood, swooned to the ground and trembled their feet. Fireflies flickered orange wings and played with a faint-hearted wind.

You stretched your legs, away from the fire. Lowered yourself into a bush near the forest. A tiny pool formed at your feet as your droplets fell. Aroused by wetness, a green snake slithered close to your big toe.

'Spirit of my fathers, bearer of good charm,' you whispered to him.

He slithered into tussocks of grass.

The bush rustled. Crouching still, you parted the leaves and peered at the night. Amber eyes peered back at you from the shrub. A leopard hissed, snarled and leapt over you. You plunged to the ground and considered for a long time his long, athletic body marked with scarlet rosettes. And you knew at once that you would bear a firstborn daughter, who would die first, and then you.

*

Everything had been put together—from the payment of a dowry of two bulls, three cows, one heifer and five roosters to the day, time and locale of your marriage—way before you saw the man to whom you were betrothed.

No wedding invitations were sent—they did not need sending. Sending invitations was stupid and a waste of time. Word of mouth carried faster and steadier than today's pieces of paper slipped in envelopes and containing a person's name. In the village, you would have to write everybody's name. Anybody not lifeless or unwell came to a wedding. Or a funeral. The whole village helped. Men brought the fish and meat. Women cooked it. They sizzled enough chicken, crisped enough pigs, tenderised enough cows, and trussed up enough spiced *pilau* rice, *mumi* fish, Nile perch and tilapia to carry a feast. People came and ate and borrowed pots to take leftovers home.

That day of your wedding, Isingoma—the man to whom you were promised—stood tall and fine-looking, his smiling lips the colour of rich berry fruit. A streak of something thrilling cloaked him, even as he drank *toggo*, pure banana beer, with the rest of the men. They sat with stretched out legs on hyacinth mats under a mango tree. A calabash of brew travelled from one man to another.

Something about the sweep of Isingoma's eyes, each time they took the direction of the stringy bark under which you sat, stirred your interest. You tried to keep your head lowered but felt inclined every now and then to lift it and wonder about your new husband.

You never felt that finger of doubt, that claw in the gut that gripped most fresh brides. Even when Isingoma took your fist—a fist because you were impatient but unprepared for his reach, finding no time to unfold your fingers into something yielding and clasping his—you never felt trapped.

You remember the old women's laughter, sharp as whistles,

and your own mother's closed face. You remember the stray dog scrounging for scraps in the courtyard, his tail wag, wagging, wagging as Isingoma led you into a newly-built hut.

You quivered at his approach, fearful of how he might initiate you into the real world of marriage. He took you masterfully, firmly. He was skilled and clinical like the fisherman he was. You submitted, because that was how you were raised: to submit. But he was also kind and affectionate in the way he brought down your shield of innocence. His touch dismissed everything you'd heard or witnessed about the formidability of men, males like your father whose approach struck only fear. What Isingoma made you feel... was not fear.

Afterwards, in soft, smoky silence that left no words behind, soft because the moon's shine was wan, and smoky because your husband had rolled up a tobacco stick and was drawing on it, Isingoma continued to caress you with his eyes. You felt fragile and whole, and just then, only then—not sooner—did you dare touch him. You reached and lightly touched that strong jaw, those smiling lips the colour of rich berries.

'Adaeze,' you said.

'It means princess,' he said.

'That's what we'll name our daughter,' you said.

Outside, the women's laughter was no longer sharp or panicked. Snug in your husband's arms, you didn't mind the mosquitoes biting the inside of your leg. You wondered if your curiosity about Isingoma would ever end, if you should tell him about the red leopard.

You were still wondering when he left just before dawn to cast his fishing net into the mist of the lake.

*

You stare at the lake—tame, green with pollution. She's sick like you became. She no longer boasts vast diversity of fish, not since the water hyacinth invaded. The free-floating menace brought devastation on trade by blocking ports. It harboured crocodiles, snakes, mosquitoes and bilharzia-carrying snails. Still, locals found use for the weed and harvested it for paper, rope, baskets, biogas, fodder and mulch. Finally, the weed died or was eradicated to something sustainable. But the lake never recovered her grace.

You remember the days of the water's beauty, centuries of history, as the lake wove her magic through the lands. She charted her course across colonies of disparate people, wooing the Bantu whose men (and sometimes women) were circumcised; the Nilotes whose gracile bodies carried tribal scarring; the Cushites, few in number, whose fairer skin and nylon hair set them apart. But people forgot their disparity to share in the offerings of the freshwater lake: her Nile perch, tilapia, pied kingfisher and silver cyprinid, fondly known and eaten as *omena*, *mukene* or *daggaa*. The lake batted her lashes, ran her feet across settlements, enamoured local communities, heartened trade.

But now, the lake is unwell. Business languishes. The village's seasons follow the water's temperament, her castings of humidity and ominous thunderheads to signal change. You remember those days, the olden days of prosperity when the once invincible African beauty was not the sick giant she now is.

*

Adaeze. Princess. She was a different kind of girl. The fastest in the village, the prettiest. She had the neck of a gazelle, the lashes of a giraffe. Adaeze could run miles, balancing a pot full of water from the lake without holding it. Not only was she the prettiest girl in the village but the brightest. Brighter than her brothers. By the time she could walk, she could charm the meat of a chicken or a goat, even tongues or gizzards, from her brothers' mouths. Her brothers never caught up with Adaeze. Even Isingoma ate from her hands.

Adaeze was a pioneer. Unable to stay indifferent, she contradicted the world of riddles and the mastery of men. She was the first woman in your family to see education. You were brought up to respect everything tradition and girls didn't go to school those days. Thankfully nowadays it was different. Then, girls learnt how to make good wives.

But, like the foreignness that came to the lake, suffocating the Nile perch, tilapia, kingfisher and *daggaa*, Christianity came to native lands. It suffocated the gods of the thorn tree and the mountain. Christians at the mission house baptised your mother and the other children's mothers, before turning to the children and their would-be spouses because, like the water weed, missionaries travelled. From when Adaeze was little, you watched the German Sister from a distance, as she taught village boys to read and write under the big mango tree. But little Adaeze didn't just watch. She sat at Sister's feet. No punishing could take her away from Sister's feet, or the learning. Finally, Sister saw and understood the stars trapped inside Adaeze and talked Isingoma into sending the child to a real school in Murutunguru.

Adaeze ran miles barefoot to and from a primary school daily and later became the first woman from the village to become a teacher. But despite being a *msomi*, educated, Adaeze stayed close to culture and men fell over themselves for her hand in marriage.

But she had her eye on Aloyse, the late Atanasi's son.

Atanasi Musiba, a friend of Isingoma's, came all the way from across the lake to beg Adaeze's hand for one of his six sons. To everyone's surprise, Isingoma let Adaeze choose. Nobody let you choose; a wedding was arranged, a man was brought and you married him. But Adaeze got to see her groom. She put a finger on his face in the picture Atanasi brought along and picked him, way before her wedding.

Aloyse had an honest face and eyes that looked at you direct. A thing about him encouraged you to trust him. He was also a *msomi*, educated like Adaeze. Together, they would see many places, travel wider than the village. You understood that the school in Murutunguru had done its work. Adaeze wanted to see the world.

She was a bridge between times, the coming of two worlds. Her eyes sought bigger, better. She hunted new places, travelled further than the village, explored. You thought of the red leopard and was happy that the green snake—spirit of your forefathers—had warded off the curse in the leopard's eye.

*

The wedding of Adaeze and Aloyse was talk of the village for days, before and afterwards. As the ceremony drew closer, hour after hour, anticipation climbed. Suddenly, that dawn, song erupted. The moment everyone was waiting for had arrived.

Dancers swished sisal skirts here, beaded shoulders there. Their toes tapped on the earth in sync to the *Ndobolo* drum. The dancers' heels made loops in the air, spraying soil each thump of the ground.

But although Adaeze's arms shone with copper and gold trinkets, she was not coated with animal fat, or wearing a sisal skirt. Her ivory gown was a gift from the mission. She looked like a queen in it. Aloyse, he wore a black suit and a tie. No villager had ever seen anything more culturally distant than that.

Unsure how to navigate their feet inside floral dresses longer than the 'Sunday bests' they wore once a week to and from church, little girls tottered along with bracelets of purple and white Jacaranda blossoms.

Aloyse had shipped in crates and crates of a strange brew called *Safari*. It came in brown bottles, not a calabash. That beer was not made for sharing: every person drank from their own bottle. People still drank it, even though it tasted like cow urine—given as medicine in finger-tip drops to babies who had the type of belly wind that pushed out bad stool and a squeal.

Villagers cheered when it was time to cut the big white cake decorated with flowers, a thing of awe that the Sisters from Murutunguru had baked. After the feasting and dancing, people watched in amusement as Aloyse carried Adaeze over his shoulder. He put her in a car, his car. When he took Adaeze away, amusement turned to fear for the children, as Aloyse's blue car bellowed like the crocodile that nearly took a child but didn't, because villagers cornered it and beat it with sticks. The crocodile's sound saved the child because the beast opened its mouth to bellow.

*

Adaeze ate dinner one night, took to bed and didn't wake up.

How does a woman, strong and healthy as a cow with milk, close her eyes and die? Before it happened, there was no terrible blackness in your heart. No thunder that roared like lions. A messenger from the boat brought news at dawn.

Coldness ran through you when you heard. You fell to your knees and howled. One single howl that lasted a small time. You sat on the ground, face covered in ash, mourners surrounding you. Their wails carried for miles and miles, and people kept coming. The sun rose high and heat jumped. Oblivious to it, women and children tore their clothes, pulled their hair, and collapsed to the ground shuddering and rolling in dirt. The men sat silent.

Grave like the men, you did not cry. You felt... drained. Adaeze was gone. Loss pain is meant to be a short, stabbing thing in the chest that brings out a wail. But this pain was too big for crying. A parent shouldn't have to bury a child. Your mourning did not finish; it kept coming back, like a memory. A bottomless knowing, long and winded, telling you that something was missing.

After they buried Adaeze, there was feasting and dancing like that of a wedding. Everyone danced, every movement symbolic. Men turned as one to face the setting sun. Powerful feet descended on the ground, again and again. Women did half a turn, rolling their shoulders to a drumbeat gone wild. Together, they celebrated death as they would life.

*

It was close to a century since you were born when you died.

The years had not been giving. Age and disease took their toll. As did the lake, you felt tired all the time. Your life ebbing, disintegrating.

Before you died, you were helpless to see. Unable to look into people's eyes, or at their hands, to find their true intentions. You understood a person from their voice and the inflection it carried. You listened to the music of words, more than their meaning, the harmony of sound, more than its source.

But you had seen much and Isingoma was a good husband. You had lived enough years together to understand each other's silences. Towards your death, you wondered if his face was wearing a strong smile or one as limp as his tread, and just as lost. You knew he needed you and worried how he would be if, if... You wondered if there was still strength in his eyes. Same honey eyes that melted you the first time you met him.

*

It's dusk. The sun, earth and moon are imperfectly aligned.

You stand holding hands with Adaeze. Together, you gaze at the lake—her pulse still beating. The moon will pass through the earth's shadow again.

'It doesn't matter about the red leopard anymore,' says Adaeze softly.

'No,' you say.

Story within a story

I yearned to write this story, born of the memories of my mother (depicted as Adaeze) and my grandmother ('you'). I set about writing it with great urgency, seeking to demystify tradition, to claim it before it could further diminish. The writing was brave, fraught with panic. What structure or direction might the narrative take? Scattered stories; whose story? In stealing it from personal history, I was able to uncloak my grandmother's story. I mended it, fabricated it, created my own pattern, decorated it with detail and wore it as mine. Her story became my story. I created a brand new design, neatly packed and speculative, from the original.

Baba Klep
Eugen Bacon

THE SKY is a royal blue and dappled with pillows of cloud, white as baby ghosts.

Today, Clyde's cleft lip palate is excruciating. His face is aflame. He's sweating agony. It's always a bad omen when pain happens, but he tries not to overthink it. The last time he felt the lip wrench, stars and shards ripping into his face—that was two years ago—his father, a vigorous baby boomer who bowled like a pro clutched his chest. He was still clutching it in a casket two days later.

Revita understands the pain. She grips Clyde's hand through it, finally smiles when he returns to himself. 'Your mama will have a fit when you bring home a black woman,' she jokes.

She's tucked behind a seatbelt stretching across a belly that's beginning to show. Her hair is long and elastic, unlike others of her tribe. She's wearing the natural glow that accompanies a pregnant woman.

Clyde's lip hurts with his smile. He looks into her chestnut eyes that go deep into his soul. Her own cleft lip is beautiful on her face. She wears it like an ornament. It's her defining feature. Hers doesn't hurt like Clyde's.

'Will you talk about my mother's fit 755 kilometres to Nairobi?'

'It's only an hour and a half of it.'

'Perhaps we should have driven.'

'I can't even…' But she's smiling.

Wells, the pilot of the UN chartered plane, roars with laughter. 'Sure,' he says with his rasp voice. 'You should have driven. All ten hours and some, all the way from Kigali. Save me a trip.'

He's a tall good-looker. Tan skin, grey eyes. A mouth you totally want to kiss. Revita said as much when she first met the young pilot.

Clyde caresses Revita's bump. 'You know I'm goofing, right? Mother will admire your intelligence. Once I tell her all you did for the people of Kigali.'

'And what good would the skills of installing, maintaining and repairing irrigation systems do in London?'

'Like teach wannabee volunteers for Africa.'

'Very useful,' she says. 'I could also teach our munchkins when they start popping out.'

Clyde's face pulls in pretend shock. 'There's more than one in there?'

They're still laughing when the four-seater suddenly rocks. Now they're swallowed in a cloud, the light plane in a seesaw. The overcast clears into a yawn of thin blue, as the sky reappears. Suddenly more cloud and the plane jerks.

'Darn,' says Wells.

'Hell's going on?' asks Clyde.

The turbulence cuts whatever answer Wells is planning. It's worse than a rocking horse. Revita's eyes close. Her fingers are clawing the armrests. Clyde is reaching for the airsick bag in the seat-back pocket when the plane judders. It tilts to the left, to the right. Now it's climbing in a tremble. Suddenly it stalls. Time is suspended. Wells is cursing like a trooper. Clyde feels, more than sees, the plane's nosing down in slow motion. Someone is screaming, and Clyde suspects it might be him. The downward rocket at full acceleration hurls his stomach up his throat. His ears are tearing. Revita is slicing his arm with her nails. He has a moment to curse the darn lip before the boom and blackness.

*

Groan. Clyde comes to. Groan. It's Revita.

She's upside-down beside him, still strapped in her seat. The air is cloudy, filling with smoke. He tries to move but is hemmed between metal and his seat. His last memory is of hands, helping hands. Then he blacks out again.

Next he comes to, someone is dragging him. Strong arms supporting his shoulders, walking, dragging, along, along.

'Wells…'

'Revita is safe,' says the white East African in his rasp voice. 'But we must move away from the plane. Sorry we had to hard land. But she's smoking and there's fuel.'

He gently lowers Clyde next to Revita.

Clyde looks around. It's bleak. Hoary dust and ash everywhere. Charcoal rock and piles of ruin.

'The hell happened here?' croaks Revita.

'Not the plane, I promise,' says jovial Wells. 'The good news is we didn't crash into Lake Victoria.'

'We're in the middle of no place,' spits Clyde.

'The flight path suggested we were nearing Entebbe when—' Wells looks around at the desolation. 'But this? What world is this?'

A burst of ululation cuts into his words. A group of children in loin cloth rushes at them. Something round hits Wells on the side of his head and knocks him out. He crumbles to the austere dust. Clyde sees the new rock's soar but is too slow to protect Revita and her head. A sound like a sigh escapes her lips. She goes limp on the ground.

A child pulls from the group, comes forth a few steps. He aims with a rock. 'No, no!' Clyde raises his arms to ward off the blow. He sees too late. It's not a rock. It's a coconut.

*

The second time he comes to, it looks like a village. There's a scatter of cinder-licked huts. They look like they endured a grave torrent of ashy rain. Grey fog in the air. Rocks and debris in piles everywhere. Something terrible happened here and the clean-up is a long-term commitment. You can see the effort. But the place looks like shit.

The children are talking in a strange language of clicks and clacks. They're animated about something. Now they're dancing and ululating around a bundle. Naked girls and babies peer from the huts. A few toddlers step out to observe the spectacle.

Clyde is roped back to back with someone. He knows without seeing it's Revita. Her soft smell of bergamot. He feels her nylon hair on his neck.

'Clyde?' she says. Her voice is small.

The toddlers flee at the sound of it.

'We'll talk to them. Sort out this mess,' he says. 'We'll tell them we're in the UN. Good people with kind hearts. That I'm a doctor and you're an irrigation expert. We can save this ghastly place from whatever doom that befell it.'

'They've taken Wells.'

'Wait until I get my hands on those little rascals—'

'They're not children, Clyde.'

'What?'

'I think they're a tribe of little people.'

*

A dance of the tribe parts to reveal Wells bound on the ground. He's naked, his mouth and eyes covered with leaves. His cries are muffled. He's trussed up like a pig on a bamboo pole. It doesn't take a genius to figure it out.

'Put him down. At once, you brutes!' But there's fear in Clyde's voice. 'Stop it. I said now!'

The tribe ignores him. They click and clack as they shoulder Wells away.

Revita's cry pulls from her toes, surges to the sky. It is like the howl of a hound.

The cleft lip suddenly attacks and tears out Clyde's face. It's possible that he faints. He stirs as the pain settles. A sweet aroma of roasting meat seeps into the air.

*

They come for him at dawn. It's still fog in the air, but a light grey one.

Clyde is in shock or despair. He doesn't struggle as they

uncouple him from Revita, as they haul him with a tug of rope to his feet. But Revita is livid. She's fighting with every inch of her living. She's snarling and thrashing, scratching and biting. Any part of her body is a weapon. Her heel connects with a jaw.

Clyde wonders how long through a roast before you die? Or do they knock you unconscious with a coconut. He's heard of superstition about albinos, how pieces of their limbs are meant to bring luck. If the tribe thinks his whiteness is albinism, will they chop something for some mythical power before they cook the rest of him? What will they take? His arms, legs, ears or genitals? But Wells was trussed whole.

He has much to say to Revita, to their unborn. He'd like to think of them as twins. He's never doubted Revita, not from the moment he saw her cleft lip in a room full of United Nations people. The connection he felt. It's like the lip reached out for her. She stood out like an African protea, radiant and thriving, regal the way she moved. She was the first woman he ever saw who never hid from a cleft lip. He thought of the Greek god Proteus, prophetic, exploratory… Clyde knew he would ride a chariot with Revita to any sun.

But she transitioned like the god, was elusive to his interest, avoided him like a turd. One day in the canteen, as he stuffed sweet potatoes and beans into his face, ravenous after a long morning of diagnosing and treating typhoid, pneumonia and malaria in babies only weeks old, Revita clapped her tray of rice and goat meat onto his table. She sat opposite him and proceeded to eat. She pulled his heart with her chestnut eyes, and he could only stare in adoration and astonishment. Finally she said, 'Your eyes and your work—they suggest you're a people lover. It so happens I'm altruistic too. But what I'm wondering is this: Are you going to propose or what?'

Now these imbeciles, unschooled carnivores, they would bloody dare to eat her and his—

Something stirs in him. He leaps with a roar. He headbutts the first one. Leaps and stamps on the next. A torso slam takes out another of the tribe. Clyde's arms are still bound behind. He flips, now on the ground. His bare feet knock out a few more shorties. The ropes give. Now he is locking with his elbows. Pulling eyes, strangling. He'll teach the half-sized philistines before they make a broth of him.

A coconut knocks him cold.

*

When he comes to, Revita is kneeling beside him. She's wiping his face with bark cloth. The little people are clicking and clacking, bowing and bowing, as if in reverence.

'The hell?' Clyde sits up with a start. Members of the tribe in the room fall away.

'Look, Clyde,' says Revita. 'Look at their lips.'

Only then does he notice. Each one has a cleft lip. Unsealed like his and Revita's.

And they are still clicking and bowing, when two women sashay in with an offering. It's a fresh roast in a calabash, some rib or thigh. Clyde and Revita are too hungry to question it.

On the last swallow, a tribesman with ash hair—perhaps an elder—appears. He claps his hands, gestures wildly.

'I think he wants us to follow him,' suggests Revita.

The elder hurries out of the hut and walks in half a trot. He keeps the distance from Clyde, as if petrified. Everywhere is ruined. It's like walking on cold lava in the dawn of a mountain's fury. They tread across bleak soil and all that fog. Now the elder is pointing at a charcoal-black statue climbing from the ground.

Revita peers long and hard at the effigy. 'I have to agree, the resemblance is uncanny.'

The gargoyle has an opening from its lip to its nose.

The elder is clicking, bowing.

'I don't know,' says Revita. 'But I could swear he's worshipping.'

Clyde laughs. 'What will they do when I start doctoring? When they see some true healing?'

'You're totally a god. And it saved you from being dinner.'

*

And so it was that Clyde and Revita lived with the tribe in no place. On the days he wondered about his widowed mother in London, how she might be doing without knowledge of her son's fate, Revita consoled him with the intensity only a person touched by the profundity of the Greek god Proteus understood.

Something else happened. Like a twist of fate. He first panicked when his cleft lip brought him to the ground in agony, but it only heralded a plague of locusts that fed the village for a month. When the lip hit his face like a hammer, a murder of crows appeared from nowhere. Nothing a well-aimed coconut couldn't fell.

As he found crude ways to cure without proper medical supplies, trusting the power of the earth and nature to restore a burn, break diarrhoea, assuage acid from gout, Clyde began to associate the agony in his lip with blessing.

So he wasn't astounded when he woke up with anguish on his face, and Revita went into labour that same day. She gave birth to one boy, not twins, and the child was cleft-lipped. Next Clyde's lip wrenched all the way to his guts, the tribe clicked and clacked, and he clicked and clacked back. It was like a miracle of Babel uncoded by a holy spirit. Suddenly he understood everything they said.

Thus, in clicks and clacks, the tribe unravelled the story of the cataclysmic event that happened before Clyde and Revita tumbled from the sky.

Two days after a millet harvest, a big bird, giant like the one that brought Clyde, Revita and the tasty one, soared in the sky. But this bird did not cartwheel to the ground. It opened its mouth and vomited light. After the light came a hiss. After the hiss, came a bellow that felled people—they died clutching their heads. When it boomed, people scattered, bits of them everywhere. A few villagers survived the bellow and the boom. Some collapsed to the fire that ravaged nearly everything. Survivors looked around, sawdust and ash everywhere. A grey world full of stumps and rock.

The branding on their face, when it happened, started without warning. One day someone noticed their lips were beginning to crack, forming a split that ran from mouth to nose. In no time, everyone was branded. It was then that they understood. The flash and boom were the work of the great god of the sky. Now He had marked them as His chosen. What they didn't understand was why He set fire to the cows and goats, sheep and cockerel. Even the maize, peas, cassava, bananas, beans, sweet potatoes and millet were gone.

Villagers fell back when they faltered into the statue. The god of the sky had lodged Himself in their midst, reincarnated as a boulder. To appease him and continue their ancestry, for indeed they would perish if they ate nothing, they sacrificed and dried the meat of newborns that arrived without a split lip.

Imagine their gratefulness, clacked the little people, when the god rewarded them with a great big tasty one from the sky. Clyde thought of the white East African's generosity, how he pulled them from the wreck.

Imagine their happiness, when it was light and they saw that the god of the sky had appeared to them in true flesh, but they were astonished He had chosen to reincarnate with no skin. They apologised completely for binding Him. Did He see how they did not harm the woman with slippery hair? Despite her charcoal face, she was made in His likeness, shaped from His ribs.

The only time they killed a tribesman with a broken lip, they clacked, he was one of them, but he was also the one who struck the god of the sky with a coconut. They served him as a fresh roast to the god, if He generously remembered.

Revita by now also understood the click language. She clicked her message to the tribe. *The god's name is Baba Cleft Lip. He's no longer angry with you.*

No? they clacked.

No. And He has absolved all your babies from sacrifice. From now on, you are not to kill or eat anyone born without a broken lip.

But, but… clicked the tribe. *What does Baba Klep suggest we eat?*

Coconuts aren't just for knocking people out, clacked Revita. *You can crack them like this. Drink their water and eat their sweet white meat.*

But, but… we can't live on coconuts alone, clicked the tribe.

Ah, yes. Baba Klep has also blessed your land, clacked Revita.
And I will show you.

Clyde needed no convincing that, between the two of
them, his wife was the brain, most shrewd. She taught the
tribe to listen for water by following locusts and birds. She
taught them to dig up the poison in the soil and separate it in
latrines. To mark and dig trenches. To make pipes of bamboo
poles, create crude but resourceful irrigation systems. Before
long, the land was lush with maize, peas, cassava, bananas,
beans, sweet potatoes and millet. It also appeared that either
the air chose to cleanse itself or the fog that wrapped around
the land had fled.

The villagers thanked Baba Klep for His goodness.

He dispersed them to scout what was left of the big bird.
They returned hauling or balancing on their heads cartons
of towels, gauze, painkillers, antimalarials, gin, beef jerky
and bars of chocolate. They pulled apart the light plane and
upgraded their irrigation pipes.

Pain coloured Baba Klep's vision, fireworks everywhere.
Revita birthed the second child. It squealed out of her womb
like a banshee, no broken lip. She suckled the tot with a
mother's poise, her world never bleak or grey.

As the sun ebbed from the birthing bed and night brooded
in, a sputter of his mother's face crossed his memory, a broken
image on a trembling screen. The shape of her jaw, the cast
of her gaze, fleeting like a chapel ghost, waiting, waiting, then
she was gone. And there was just his wife and newborn. He
wondered if he'd ever know that he'd stayed too long, and
when that happened if he could ever leave. He stared at the
facts, the taste of a muddy river in his mouth.

Story within a story

I aimed this story for an anthology, but it crawled out like an African octopus with a mind of its own. I sought to capture an apocalypse survival fiction whose protagonist was a person with a disability. Where Clyde wears his cleft lip as an inconvenience from the agony it causes him, Revita (the quiet strength in the story) adorns hers, it's part of her beauty. A disastrous crash catapults them into a tribe getting back on its feet after a post-apocalyptic event, and our two protagonists become part of creating a new, sustainable solution.

Ancestry
Eugen Bacon

TAP! TAP! jig! roll-a-hip! jig!

Adisa watches the Bafazi dancers. One fair woman, she has the big lashy eyes of a *nyala*—the white striped gazelle with a pale coat—spits each time Adisa catches her eye.

Only moments ago, it seemed, the Bafazi raced with Adisa into the night. She was gagged with leaves, slung over one man's shoulder. Jeru. Now he's seated to her right on the gazebo near a popping fire. He puffs himself, picks at dried mucus along the plateau of his nostril, right near a wart.

'Spirit,' he says, and reaches to stroke her chin with those grimed hands.

Adisa hisses.

'That I love about you.' Spittle squirts from his mouth. He's missing incisors. 'But I'll tame you.'

Adisa spits near his feet. 'We'll see.'

His glee is more rasp than laugh. He rocks, almost collapses into the flames. He's big like a toad, shaped like a toad, and—with bulge of eyes and pockmarked skin coated with red dye—truly resembles a river toad.

She glowers at the lust in his eyes. 'Only a coward steals a woman. Do I look like a goat to you?'

'Would your father have given me your hand?'

'Never to Bafazi filth.'

'Aysh.'

'And Father already has chosen another. *More* worthy.' Daggers in her eyes.

'But tonight I will take you, swell you with my babies. Even him, your worthy one, he cannot undo this.'

'It's *her*. My worthy one is a woman. What do you know of my people?'

'The Modo?' He's pensive for a moment. Then laughs. 'A curious lot. But I know enough to ask if you'll call our children Bafazi filth?'

The drums become soulful, distant. Jeru is now steamy drunk, filled with pride and liquor made from black bee honey. He pokes out toad hands, warms them above glowing coals.

'Your clan has ruined you,' he says. 'Cheer up, beautiful one. You'll soon know what it's like to be with a man.' His burst of ribald laughter.

The soft curtain of Adisa's dark braids conceals her eyes as she stares unblinking at the pulsing dusk. Her Modo people counted on her. What happens now?

Jeru's gaze runs along the toga that cuts across her shoulder. He flicks a tongue over his lip. The rise in his loin cloth discloses his desire. She reads his mind. He thinks he can take her now, drag her into the bush, break her reluctance. But the night is young, rife with melody. He clears his throat, spits phlegm into crackling flames.

With impulse he tears himself from the ground. His legs, disinclined to leave newfound bounty but altogether entranced by the music, walk in different directions. The loin cloth loosens from his waist. It slips to the ground, overwhelmed by a distended belly stuffed with gizzard and yam. He dances, oblivious to his nakedness, sways to the rest of his clan.

The woman, Nyala, gyrates her hips towards him.

Adisa stretches her legs away from the fire. She listens as needles in the nerves of her toes die away. She rises, watches Jeru's shudder dance. He half-limps, half-squats, taps the ground with his heel.

Adisa's beaded ornaments tinkle with motion. Nyala looks over her shoulder, continues dancing. More eyes of dancers follow Adisa. They abandon interest when she feigns a call of nature in the undergrowth. Beyond the village, a forest filled with creatures. Spirits circle overhead, daring this stolen bride to escape now, because daylight is not an option.

But what she seeks is more than escape. She looks at the dancers. *Tap! Tap! Jig! Roll-A-Hip! Jig!* She has a mission for her people. In a neon hue of orange, the moon smiles young and soft.

Adisa approaches Jeru. The gleam in his eyes. 'Come to your senses?'

She breaks into a smile, reaches with both hands. He grabs them, presses them with clammy palms to his shoulders. He paws her breasts, her hips, as they dance. She brushes her lips along his ear, whispers: 'Someone forget to tell you about the ancestral weapon of the Modo people.'

'What weapon?'

'This one.' She plunges a fist through his chest, tears his heart out in a spurt of blood. 'Adisa means grave. I come from ancient stock.'

The Bafazi scatter with shrieks, scramble for the forest.

Adisa laughs as she picks them one by one. Dusk swallows

her litheness. Owl eyes light her path. She loops a tree, chases Nyala who cries her death into the darkness. Adisa rips with bare hands the spine from the woman's back.

Her carnage… First it is rage, then thrill. Now it's hunger. She gains on those who jump down a small valley, into the open plain where the forest peels back from a whistling wind.

She falls on a screaming warrior, pulls out her fangs and feeds.

Story within a story

In this maiden-in-distress story, I sought to explore the marginalization of females in third world countries, examining how patriarchal attitudes, practices and behaviour restrict the destinies of girls and women. 'Ancestry' also satisfies a curiosity to write vampire noire.

Carnival
Milton Davis

Antwon was late. He rushed out his Peachtree Street flat as he summoned a Rideout and the electric transport appeared moments later, scanning the young mixer for his ID and payment. Antwon jumped in and the door closed.

"King Center Art Gallery," he said. 'High priority.'

"Insufficient credit," the car replied.

Antwon slammed his fist on the empty seat.

"Scan for ride share options," he said.

The car hummed before answering.

"Ride share confirmed. Please buckle your seat belt and thank you for choosing Rideout for your transportation needs."

Antwon buckled up then leaned back into his seat, pissed. The latest song by Prince, Inc. filled the cabin as the Rideout lifted into aerial traffic. If his account was short that meant Antwon's payment didn't go through. That was the second time. There wouldn't be a third.

He tapped his band and the holoscreen hovered before his eyes.

"Damarius Taylor," he said.

The screen pulsed for a moment before Damarius appeared, a wide grin on his brown bearded face.

"There he is!" Damarius said. "Man, this shit is ice!"

Damarius took off his shirt, then extended his muscular arms. His tats illuminated then danced about his body. Antwon grinned. He did do good work. He tapped his band and the tats went dark. Damarius looked stunned.

"What the fuck?"

"Dee, where's my cred?"

Damarius was still staring at his torso.

"Your what? What the hell just happened?"

"Mufa where's my cred?" Antwon shouted.

Damarius glared at Antwon. "You shut me down? You shut me down! Man, I paid your ass!"

"My account is short the same amount you owe. You didn't pay me kaka."

"Quit fucking with me Twon," Damarius said. "I made the trans while you were walking out the door!"

"I'm not arguing with you, bwoi." Antwon shut down the comm. The Rideout rose to the fifth level then eased down on a condo plat. The door slipped open and an umber woman wearing a tight-fitting kente dress and matching headwrap entered the lift and sat beside him.

"Piedmont District," the woman said.

"Thank you for choosing Rideout," the lift responded. The door closed and the lift maneuvered into the swirling traffic.

"Nice outfit," Antwon said.

The woman turned to him and smiled.

"Thank you... oh my ancestors! Antwon Green!" The woman squealed then clapped her hands. "I'm sharing a lift with Twon the Don!"

No matter how many times it happened Antwon was always flattered and somewhat embarrassed when people recognized him. The woman opened her purse and her phone emerged, rising over her head.

"Look y'all! I'm riding a lift with Twon the Don!"

Antwon waved. "Hello friends of the woman in the fiya dress."

"Kecia," the woman said. "My name is Kecia Thomas. I was at your Solstice set two years ago. It was my life!"

"I'm glad you enjoyed it. It was hot."

"So, what you doing for Carnival?" Kecia asked.

"Can't tell you," Antwon replied. "All I can say is that it will be unforgettable."

"Better than Solstice?"

Antwon smiled. "Life ending."

"Piedmont District" the lift announced.

Kecia opened her purse and her phone descended into it. They stared at each other in silence. Kecia finally blushed.

"This is my stop," she said.

"Yes, it is," Antwon replied.

"You know, my plans are flexible."

Antwon laughed. "Mine aren't. It was nice meeting you, Kecia."

Kecia lunged at him, wrapping him in a tight hug. She smelled of mangoes.

"You are so ice!" she said. "I can't wait to see what you do for Carnival!"

The lift door slid open and Kecia climbed out of the lift.

"You have a nice day, Kecia," Antwon said.

Kecia waved as the lift door closed. Antwon's phone buzzed; he looked at it and saw Kecia's number. He quickly deleted it. The phone buzzed again and Damarius's face appeared.

"Check your account," he said.

Antwon punched up his account. The creds were there.

"Thank you, bwoi," Antwon said.

"Now turn my tats back on," Damarius said. "I got a date tonight."

"Done," Antwon said. "And never call me again."

Damarius's eyes went wide. "Wait, bruh! You ain't gonna..."

Antwon cut him off, deleted his number and blocked him.

"Broke ass," he whispered.

The Rideout descended to ground level, landing wheels dropping as it touched pavement. It rolled to a stop before the King Center Art Gallery.

"Thank you for choosing Rideout," the car said. "Have a blessed day."

Antwon skipped to the Center door, which slid open when it recognized his ID.

"Twon!"

Marissa jogged up to him and gave him a warm hug and a quick dap.

"You're late," she said as she passed him a joint. Twon took a deep toke then coughed.

"Shit! Where'd you get this?"

"Rocky Mountains Hydro," Marissa answered. "Only the best for the best."

She grabbed his arm then dragged him across the gym floor to the dance hall.

"Kye and Dame have been going at it since daybreak," she said. "They killing it."

She extended the joint to Antwon and he waved it away.

One drag and he was probably going to be high the rest of the week. When he entered the dance hall he smiled. The room shook with old school soca and like Marissa said, Kye and Dame were killing it. He almost began dancing but didn't. He was as bad a dancer as he was a good DJ, and he was the best DJ in the world.

He watched them dance for few more minutes, his smile matching his high. Kye and Dame were money well spent. Carnival was going to be so ice.

Kye was spinning when she saw him. She stopped then glared at him.

"Music off," she said. "Where have you been?"

Antwon walked toward Kye; his arms outstretched for a hug. Kye hit him in the chest with the palm of her hand.

"Where are our costumes?" she said.

Antwon dropped his arms to his side and made an exaggerated sad face.

"What? I've been waiting all day... oomph!"

Kye hit him in the chest again, this time harder.

"Stop playing with me," she said. "We're only a month away from Carnival. We should be dancing in our costumes right now. And what about the holos? I hope we didn't get these implants for nothing."

"The costumes are on the way," Antwon promised. "I talked to JaBarr and Dean two days ago and they're almost done. As for the holos, let's see how they work."

A smile broke like sunshine on Kye's face.

"Put on your skins," Antwon said.

Kye skittered across the floor, grabbed Dame then dragged him into the dressing room. They returned moment later, the dance skins clinging to their every contour. Antwon lost concentration staring at Kye's perfection. Her hands went to her hips and she frowned.

"Twon, concentrate," she said.

"What... oh yeah, right. Lights!"

The lights dimmed. Antwon pulled up his shirt sleeve, revealing his touchpad on his forearm. It was old school, but Antwon liked tapping the screen in time with the music. This task, however, didn't require rhythm. He punched in the code and the holo costumes appeared. Marissa almost dropped her joint.

"Ice!" she exclaimed.

Kye and Dame hurried to the nearest mirror.

"What do you think?" Antwon said.

Kye shrugged. "It's alright. I've seen Trinnies with better."

Antwon grinned. He knew Kye was going to say that.

"Music," he said.

Kye and Dame took the queue. They danced, the holo-costumes synching with their every move. Antwon tapped the buttons and the costumes changed colours in rhythm with the music. He saw a smile come to Kye's face.

"This is better," she called out. "Can't win with this, though."

"You haven't seen it all," Antwon called back.

"When?" Dame said.

"Carnival."

Kye and Dame kept dancing with angry faces. Antwon laughed.

"Don't worry. It will be amazing. You just keep doing what you're doing. I'll handle the rest."

He swiped his hand over the pad, sharing the code with Kye.

"Keep practising. I'll be back in a few days."

"Where are you going?" Dame asked.

Antwon looked at Marissa. "Where am I going?"

"Mile High," Marissa answered.

"Really? Ice!"

"Mile High!" he yelled out as he and Marissa walked away.
He turned back to Marissa.

"She's in Mile High? You sure?"

Marissa shook her head. "No. Nothing's sure with her. It's
the best lead I got. The note said go to Mile High. Once you
get there check into the Snowcap Hotel. She'll find you from
there. If she wants to."

Antwon gave Marissa dap. "I owe you."

Marissa grabbed his arm. "Hey, why don't I come with
you? We can finish this." She patted her pants pocket.

"Not tonight," Antwon said. "I got to lay some tracks
tonight then pack. Rain check, okay?"

Marissa looked crestfallen. "Okay, cool. Next time."

"Solid."

Antwon summoned a Rideout as he left the building. He
laughed out loud as he waited; if Marissa came to his flat with
weed and let those dreads out there would be no tracks and
no Mile High, at least for three days. He couldn't be distracted.
Everything was about Carnival.

He jumped into the Rideout to his building. Antwon
moved two years ago when his former flat became too small.
He needed more terabytes for his business and the burb flats
didn't have the capacity. So, he put in a request for a Flat in the
Pit. He thought it would take longer than it did, but celebrity
has its privileges. The Rideout dropped him off and security
scanned him in. Seconds later he was on the 52nd floor

bouncing to his room, the tracks floating together in his head. By the time he entered his flat, he had at least three tracks. He didn't make it to the bedroom, dropping everything on the floor as he went directly to his tables. His fingers flowed across the board, the music running like sweet water. It was going to be a long, beautiful night.

*

Antwon's alarm shoved him out of bed at exactly 12:30 pm. He lay still, his eyes opening to the graffiti mural on his ceiling. Last night's session went way too long, but he was feeling it and couldn't let go. And Marissa showed up anyway. There was no saying no to her, especially with her dreads loose. He sat up to look at his bed then smirked. Marissa was gone; the only sign of her the lingering smell of weed and cocoa butter.

Antwon stumbled to the shower. He called up the Tube schedule to Mile High as he showered. He had two hours before the next ride, which was plenty of time. The jets dried him as he called up last night's mixes then swiped them to his waiting clients. The crypts showed up in his account seconds later. He was looking in his closet debating whether to pack or buy clothes when he got to Mile High when his forearm buzzed. It was Kye.

"What's up, beautiful?"

"Hey, handsome. Me and Dame were up all night working on the routine. We made a few changes."

Kye's image was replaced with the duo working it out, holo-costumes and all. Antwon's eyes teared up.

"That's amazing," he said.

"It could be even more amazing if I knew what to expect

at Carnival," she said.

"Just keep doing what you're doing," Antwon said. "It will all come together. I promise."

"C'mon Antwon!" Kye pleaded. "Give me something!"

"Can't," Antwon said. "Trust me."

Kye scowled then broke contact. Antwon shook his head. He wanted to tell her; hell, he wanted to tell everybody. But there was no such thing as a secret once a word's been spoken. Truth was he didn't know if things would come together. He wouldn't know until he went to Mile High.

Antwon arrived at the Tube ten minutes before departure with a small bag. He decided he didn't want to take the time to shop, and who knew what the trends in Mile High were, and he was not going to be tacky. Each Urb had its own flavour, and Antwon preferred Aytee-El's.

The tube was crowded but not packed. Antwon killed the four hours working on new mixes and tracks, ignoring the people staring at him and trying to get his attention. He was relieved when they reached Mile High. He rushed to the exit with his single bag and jumped on the escalator to the surface. He was greeted by a stunning view of the snow-capped Rockies. In five more years, if all went well, people would one day be able to visit them again. Antwon was looking forward to it.

He pulled up directions to the Snowcap Hotel while paging a Rideout when the signal was interrupted. A face filled the screen; a brown-skinned woman wearing hoop earrings and shades with a flowered headwrap smiled at him.

"Hi Antwon. Welcome to Mile High. There's been a change of plans. I need you to go to the Environmental Transition Office. A Rideout is on its way to pick you up."

"How do I know this is legit?" Antwon asked.

The woman smiled. "You don't. But you've come this far. You might as well go all the way."

Antwon was about to reply when the Rideout appeared.

"Fleek!" Antwon whispered as he climbed inside.

"Welcome to Mile High, Antwon Green. Thank you for choosing Rideout."

The Rideout whisked him to the city. Antwon was disappointed he didn't have time to sightsee, but he was there for business, possibly the most important business of his life. Carnival was always important; it was the biggest audience for his skills. But this one was special. He was betting all on this one, and he was in the Mile High to make sure it was beyond his best.

The Rideout climbed to high traffic as it continued through Mile High. They were passing through the main city and into the urbs. Antwon drummed his fingers on his thigh. Where exactly was this thing taking him?

"Rideout, confirm destination," he said.

"That information is confidential," the EV replied.

"Confidential? What the fleek do you mean confidential?"

"The renter has requested that the location remain confidential. If you feel threatened, you can terminate the service at any time."

It was decision time. If he walked away Carnival was fleeked. If he stayed Carnival still might be fleeked. He threw up his hands then slumped in his seat.

The Rideout took him to the skirts, landing before a small windowless square building. The door lifted and Antwon was blasted with frigid air.

"Thank you for choosing Rideout. Have a blessed day."

Antwon took his bag and stepped out the EV. He was so cold he shook.

"Somebody needs to turn it up!" he shouted.

The door to the square building open and a woman he recognized from his cell emerged. She ambled up to Antwon, extending her hand.

"Antwon Green?" she asked.

"The one and only."

"I'm Kadisha Simone. Follow me."

"Where are we going?" Antwon asked.

"Outside," Kadisha replied.

Antwon laughed. "Yeah, right. Look Kadisha, I didn't come all the way here to play games. Just take me to Set. We got business."

"If you want to meet Set, we have to go Outside."

Antwon stopped. "We can't! Rangers only, remember? What kind of krak is this?"

"I'm a ranger," Kadisha said. "So is Set. And today, you are, too."

Kadisha entered the building. Antwon didn't move.

"Antwon?" Kadisha called out. "You're wasting time. I thought you didn't want to do that."

"Fleek!" he said. "Fleek, fleek, fleek!"

He picked up his bag and followed Kadisha into the building.

"Here." Kadisha swiped her forearm and his cell vibrated.

"What did you just give me?" Antwon asked.

"Credentials."

The inside of the building was sparse, a few scattered chairs with screens displaying scrolling images of Outside landscapes.

"What is this place?" Antwon asked.

"Excursion travel centre," Kadisha replied. "I take it by your question you're not a fan of Outside."

"Never had a reason to be," Antwon replied.

Kadisha sighed. "Typical."

"What?"

"Nothing."

They reached a door at the end of the building. A light flashed and the door slid open. Antwon could see the landscape over Kadisha's shoulder. He tried to move his feet but couldn't. Kadisha turned around.

"What are you waiting for?"

"I've never been Outside," Antwon confessed.

Kadisha rolled her eyes. "Gods!"

She grabbed Antwon's arm then dragged him through the door. The cold air hit him, and he shivered. Kadisha looked at him and sucked her teeth.

"It's warm in the EV," she said.

Antwon bolted to the vehicle, opened the door then jumped inside. Kadisha climbed inside, taking the front seat. She pressed a button on the console and the EV came to life. Antwon watched puzzled as she grasped the circular object in front of her.

"What are you doing?" he asked.

"Driving," Kadisha replied.

"What?"

Kadisha pivoted around then chuckled.

"I'm driving," she said. "None of that self-steering stuff on the Outside."

Antwon swallowed. "Is that safe?"

"Sometimes," Kadisha replied. "It gets interesting when

the weather gets bad."

She turned around then pulled out on the road. Antwon made sure his seatbelt was fastened as he waited for the EV to lift off. Five minutes later they were still rolling on the ground.

"Is this thing broken?" he asked. "We're still on the ground."

"It doesn't fly," Kadisha answered. "We're restricted to ground travel near Mile High. Airborne EVs are only used to reach remote areas."

The rocking over the uneven ground was making Antwon queasy. He held his stomach.

"Don't throw up in my ride," Kadisha said. "We're almost home."

They rolled over a wooded hill. As they crested, Kadisha's home came into view. The cube shaped structure looked like someone had torn a flat from Mile High and dropped it in the forest. Antwon let out a sigh when Kadisha pulled next to the building and shut off the EV.

"Home," she said.

Antwon followed Kadisha into the home. It was a one-room studio with a large patterned rug in the centre. Antwon was expecting to see something resembling the old Westerns he watched on the pirate channel, but Kadisha's flat was nothing unusual. She pulled a chair from the small dining table then sat.

"So, what do you want from me?" she said.

Antwon sat. "I don't want anything from you, except taking me to Set. When will we do that?"

Kadisha smiled. "You're talking to her."

Antwon gasped. "You? You're Set?"

Kadisha nodded. "Talk fast. If I'm not convinced in five

minutes the answer is no."

Antwon stuck his hand into his pocket and pulled out an object. He tossed it to Kadisha.

"I don't need to say a word. Everything is on this."

Kadisha frowned. "You brought me a file on a flash drive? I didn't think these existed on the Inside."

"Took me a fortune to get that one."

"Why?"

Antwon smiled. "Because we both know there are no secrets in the cloud."

Kadisha grinned. "Smart man. Let's see what we got."

Kadisha tapped the tabletop and a panel slid open. She inserted the flash drive into the port.

"Screen," she said.

Code filled the space over the table. Kadisha reached into the hidden compartment, pulled out a pair of VR specs then put them on. She studied the code then whistled.

"You got some skills," she said.

It took everything in Antwon's power to keep from jumping to his feet and pumping his fist. A compliment from Set/Kadisha was nothing to take lightly.

"Thanks. So, what do you think?"

Kadisha removed the specs. "This is buck wild crazy. Most of this is theory, and if it does work, you will have broken so many laws I don't think you'll ever see the light of day again."

"But is it possible?"

Kadisha made a sly grin. "Yes."

"So, you'll do it?"

"Yes, but for twice of what you're offering."

Antwon's hand slapped his forehead. "Twice? Fleek!"

"Hey, this is some serious dope," Kadisha said. "I'll have

to change my life if this works. You will, too. Which leads me to ask, why are you doing this? You're the top DJ in Aytee-El and one of the best on the grid. You don't need this."

"Why do you hack?" Antwon asked.

Kadisha smiled. "Because I can."

Antwon grinned. "Same reason."

"Yeah, but you're set," Kadisha replied. "I can screw something up then hide. I'm adaptable. You're plugged in. You might lose everything."

"It's the challenge," Antwon said. "I didn't get here by being safe. I take chances all the time. I push the boundaries every opportunity I get. And when it works, the rush is incredible. There's nothing like it. Not even sex."

"That's debatable," Kadisha said. She stood then strolled to her fridge. "You want something to drink?"

"You got rum?"

"No, but I got wine."

"That'll do."

Kadisha took a bottle of red wine from her cabinet and poured them both a glass. She handed a glass to Antwon.

"Let's go out back," she said.

"It's cold out there!" Antwon protested.

Kadisha went into her closet and emerged with two heavy woollen blankets. She tossed one to Antwon then exited the back door. Antwon wrapped the blanket around his shoulders then followed Kadisha out onto the small patio. They sat in cushioned chairs, a small table between them. Kadisha took a sip of wine then sat her glass on the table. Antwon did the same. He stared at Kadisha, waiting for her to restart their conversation.

"Don't look at me," she said. "Look at them."

"Who?"

"Not who, what." She pointed to the snow-topped mountains. Antwon glanced at them.

"Okay, I looked. Now can we finish... ?"

"Shhh," Kadisha said. "Drink your wine and look. I'm thinking."

Antwon slumped in his chair then sipped his wine. The blanket did a good job keeping him warm. He stared into the distance, focusing on the mountains. They were beautiful; towering higher than anything humans had yet to build. The quiet was unnerving at first, but as he settled in, he realized it was quite calming. He saw something drifting in the sky and thought for a moment it was an EV. It wasn't, of course. It was some kind of bird. He sat up, straining his eyes trying to make out the details. Motion out the corner of his eye caught his attention; he looked in the woods before him to see a four-legged beast come into view. It looked at them briefly then began munching the grass in the clearing.

"I'll do it."

Antwon jumped. "What?"

Kadisha smiled. "I'll do it. I'll meet you in Aytee-EL in two days."

Antwon was elated and concerned at the same time.

"Two days? We need to get started now."

"Two days," Kadisha said. "I'll contact you when I arrive. We're not to be together unless it's absolutely necessary."

"You say I got skills, right? It took me a long time to develop this code. I can be useful."

Kadisha grinned. "I'm much better than you. That's why you're here. Two days. Now finish your wine and I'll take you back to Mile High."

They sat in silence as they finished their wine. Nature had its effect on Antwon the longer he observed it. It was truly beautiful.

"You think they'll let us out again?" he asked.

"I hope not," Kadisha answered. "We almost killed everything the last time."

"But we're different now."

Kadisha laughed. "No, we're not. I'm a ranger, remember? Every day we catch somebody trying to cut down a tree, murder an animal, or dump a toxin in a river just for the hell of it. Mother Earth won't survive a second round of us. So, we stay on the Inside. That's the law."

"I don't know," Antwon said. "I mean, we're part of nature, too."

"We stopped being a part of nature when our greed overtook our common sense," Kadisha said. "We're a cancer determined to kill our host and we've been quarantined, not cured. It's going to take a few more generations for that."

Kadisha turned up her glass, finishing her wine.

"Let's get you back to civilization."

Antwon took one last look at the mountains then followed Kadisha inside. The ride back to Mile High was subdued; Kadisha was silent, Antwon kept looking back at the mountainous landscape. The sun was setting behind the western peaks as they reached the transition building, the city lights awakening to challenge the encroaching darkness. Kadisha held the door open to the city for him.

"Two days," she said. "I expect the first half of the payment in my account by the time I get back to my house. Otherwise the deal is dead."

Antwon's fingers ran across his forearm. Kadisha glanced

away then back to him.

"Thank you. It's still early. Mile High is lively at night. Nothing like Aytee-El, but you might find something to do."

"Right," Antwon said. "See you in two days."

Antwon hailed an EV. The vehicle descended and he stepped inside, his mood sour. He thought he'd be happy; Set said yes, which mean Carnival was going to be spectacular. But his mood had nothing to do with the celebration. It was sitting Outside, looking at the mountains, experiencing something that he might never see again that took him down. He needed cheering up.

"City guide," he said.

A holomap of Mile High appeared before him. He racked his brain, trying to remember the name of the rave Marissa told him about. He squinted his eyes and it popped in his head.

"Juke!" he said. "Take me to Juke."

The EV lifted then weaved through the hi-rises, touching down in the Mile-High entertainment district. Antwon heard Juke before he saw the flashing old-fashion neon sign mounted over the rave entrance. A line of people snaked from the entrance and around the building for two blocks. Antwon climbed out of the EV then strolled to the entrance. He usually kept his profile incognito, but tonight he decided to be a celebrity. A quick brush of his forearm and he was exposed. The security drones hovering over the crowd pivoted toward him, their green LEDs flashing. Before the crowd could surge toward him the heavies arrived, forming a circle of muscles and suits around him. One of the guards, a brown-skinned man as wide as he was tall, lowered his shades and he smiled.

"Twon the Don in Mile High? Ice! I'm Bruno Bruiser.

Follow me."

The heavies pushed through the throng and into the rave. Antwon was showered with pulsing bass and lights. He was feeling better already. The heavies took him to the DJ booth, where a straw blonde woman wearing a neon orange jumpsuit greeted him with a joyful smile.

"Twon the Don! To what do I owe this privilege?

"Roxy Row!" Twon replied. "I didn't know this was your spot."

They did the Jay dap then hugged.

"Only been here two weeks," Roxy said. "Dooley's got stingy, so I bounced. You bring your shit?"

"Always," Antwon replied.

Antwon punched his code then swiped his forearm. His holoboard appeared next to Roxy's set up.

"Epic!" Roxy shouted. "Let's do a tag team!"

The boards synced and it was on. Roxy and Antwon went beat for beat, mixing into each other's selections and remixing on the breaks. The crowd felt the energy and responded; their dancing more vigorous. It had been a long time since Antwon did a duo session and he was reminded how much he missed it. As they mixed he captured snippets of beats from each song, familiarizing himself with the Mile-High groove. Every city had a groove; a little something their inhabitants responded to. In the Aytee-El they called it Durty; in Queen City they called it Bop. Antwon didn't know what it was called in Mile High, but he was about to find out.

"You're about to do it, aren't you?" Roxy said.

Antwon answered with a smirk and a wink.

Roxy punched the air. "Shit yeah!" She swiped her holoboard away. "Don't start until I'm on the floor."

Antwon gave Roxy the thumbs up and she hurried out the booth. Antwon continued to harvest the beats until he saw her stepping into the crowd. Antwon turned on the mic.

"Mile High, how you feeling?"

The crowd answered with a roar. Antwon grinned.

"Twon the Don on the boards tonight," he said. "And it's about to go down!"

Twon went freestyle and the crowd exploded. This was his domain, the vibe he was known for. As he layered the beats, he watched the crowd, feeding off their energy. Seconds later they were zoning, deep into the perfect moment of give and take.

"Are you with me!?" he shouted.

"Yeah!" the crowd back.

"Are you with me?"

"Yeah!"

"Then show me!"

Antwon switch into deep bass breakdown and the crowd responded.

"This is brand new, y'all!" he said. "It's called the Mile-High Durty!"

Antwon glanced up; camera drones jostled outside the deejay booth window. He grinned, flashed a peace sign, then went back to work. Antwon lost track of time; when the lights flickered for last call it caught him by surprise.

Roxy entered the booth, her eyes wide with wonder.

"That was hot as fleek!"

She swiped her forearm and her holoboard reappeared. Antwon closed out his board.

"Thanks for letting me spin," he said. "I needed it."

Roxy tapped her board. Fifteen hundred crypts downloaded

into his account.

"Hey, you didn't need to do that," he said.

"You know how much I'm going to make on residual feeds?" she said. "This set has 2mil views already."

"What time is it?" Antwon asked.

"Six a.m."

"Fleek! Gotta go. My Bullet leaves at 7:30."

Antwon gave Roxy dap then hurried away.

"Let me know when you come to the A," he shouted. "We can do this again."

"Will do!" Roxy shouted back.

"If I'm not in prison," Antwon whispered.

The crowd had dispersed when he went outside. A few folks asked for his autograph which he obliged before calling a Rideout. He hopped in and the EV whisked him to the Tube terminal. Antwon used extra crypts to upgrade his seat to private on the way to the station. He worked his way to his Bullet and to the VIP cubes. Once inside the plush compartment he jumped on the bed, closed his eyes and fell asleep.

*

"Welcome to Aytee-El."

Antwon sat up and rubbed his eyes. His cabin pulsed with baby blue light while the local news played on the vid. First level riders got the privilege to disembark first, but Antwon decided to grab a few extra minutes of sleep by waiting until the bullet was empty.

"Mr. Pierce?"

Antwon woke up a second time to the pleasant face of a bullet steward on his screen.

"We have to ask you to leave the bullet. We can't board new passengers until the train is empty.

"My bad," Antwon said. He gathered his things then hurried off the train. He walked with the throng to the Metro, and then hopped on for the twenty-minute ride into the Pit. As he rode the Peachtree Station escalator to the surface, the details of his trip to Mile-High rolled around in his head. Spending that short time Outside affected him more than he realised. The more he thought about it, the more it worried him. He was so immersed he didn't notice he'd reached the top of the escalator.

"Sir?"

Antwon turned to see an attractive woman smiling at him.

"Yes?"

"You're blocking the escalator."

"What... oh, I'm sorry."

He stepped aside, freeing the others to go about their daily business. He shook his head clear then called up Marissa. Her bright face filled his view.

"Morning, love," she said. "Back from Mile High?"

"Yep."

"Saw you set last night on the wave. Ice!"

"Thanks. How's the prep going?"

"Great, but Kye and Dame are still bitching. They want to know what you got planned. Krak, I want to know what you got planned."

"All in good time," Antwon replied.

Marissa gave him that special smile. "Can I come over?"

Antwon chuckled. "I got to get to the crib and get some sleep. I'll meet y'all at the centre around fourteen hundred. After that, we'll see. Ice?"

"Ice."

Antwon was only a few blocks from his condo, so he decided to walk the rest of the way. He was walking up to the entrance when his phone buzzed.

"Speak."

Kadisha's face appeared.

"Change of plans," she said. "I'll be in Aytee-El tomorrow morning."

"What's the matter?"

"I need to get into the ADOT."

Antwon ran his hand over his head. "Really? The code was written to work externally."

"It won't," Kadisha replied. "And don't ask me if I'm sure. I am."

"I don't know," Antwon replied. "The ADOT? That's heavy security."

"Don't worry about that," Kadisha said. "Meet me at the station at oh seven hundred."

Antwon scratched his head. "Wow, Kadisha. I don't know."

"You want your Carnival?" she asked.

"Of course, I do."

"Then meet me at seven," Kadisha said. "Otherwise it's not happening."

Kadisha cut him off. Antwon continued to stare where her face had been, his mind tumbling. This was serious shit. Breaking into a government facility? That was serious.

Antwon was so preoccupied he walked by his condo. He wandered the streets for an hour, going over the code. Hunger pangs hit him, and he worked his way to Piedmont Park then bought a loaded sausage dog from the Weiner King food truck. He sat on a nearby bench, absently eating as code filled his head. Then he saw it.

"Fleek!"

He threw away the rest of the sausage dog and jogged to his condo. He spent the rest of the day and most of the night trying to fix the code, but by the time the sun rose over the city he gave up. Kadisha was right. They had to go in.

His cell buzzed and he sighed. He punched his forearm and Kadisha's face filled the screen.

"I'm here," she said.

"I'm on my way," he replied.

"Don't bother. I'll be there in a few."

"Wait! What?"

The screen went blank. Antwon scrambled to clean up his condo before her arrival, not wanting to appear the slob he was. Fifteen minutes later the door buzzed, and he let Kadisha in.

"Hey! What's..."

Kadisha handed him a clothes box.

"Get dressed. Where's your bathroom?"

"Down the hall," he said as he took the box. Kadisha nodded then marched to the bathroom. Antwon went to his bedroom and opened the box. Inside was an Aytee-EL DOT uniform.

"Oh shit," he said.

"You dressed yet?" Kadisha called out from the bathroom.

"Almost," Antwon called out. He undressed and put on the uniform. When he turned around Kadisha stood in his bedroom door, her hand extended. In it was an ADOT employee badge.

"Um, did you see me in my..."

'Boy please. Let's go," she said.

She turned then strode for the door. Antwon ran behind her.

"Why such a hurry? Can't we talk about this?"

"We have a small window of opportunity," Kadisha replied. "We can talk on the way."

Antwon followed Kadisha to the street. A Rideout appeared and they climbed in.

"I assume you found the error?" Kadisha asked.

"Yeah," Antwon said. "I tried..."

"I could kick myself for missing it," Kadisha said, cutting him off. "If I'd seen it sooner, I would have turned you down."

Antwon's eyes widened. "Is it that bad?"

"Look at us," she answered. "It's that bad."

Antwon and Kadisha hurried from the condo to the streets. Antwon summoned a Rideout.

"Aytee..."

"No," Kadisha interjected. "Rising Star Restaurant."

Antwon gave Kadisha a questioning look.

"It's a popular restaurant for ADOT employees," she said. "We'll walk from there."

"How do you know all this?" Antwon asked.

Kadisha smirked. "You really have to ask?"

The Rideout whisked them to Rising Star, a small breakfast spot on the corner of Ellis and Vine. Antwon's stomach rumbled as they entered. He didn't have breakfast. He was eyeing a delicious looking sausage sandwich when Kadisha turned him about.

"No time for that," she said. "Let's go."

They walked with a group of ADOT workers to the building. The workers chatted with each other while glancing at Kadisha and Antwon. A few shared smiles; some looked at them suspiciously. One woman in particular kept staring at Antwon, her face scrunched up in that way people do when trying to remember someone. Her eyes went wide and a big grin appeared on her face.

"Twon the Don!" she exclaimed.

"Sheeit!" Antwon said under his breath.

The woman made her way to him.

"You look just like him," she said.

"Who?" Antwon said.

"Twon the Don. I was just rocking off one of his vids yesterday. He's so cool."

Kadisha came and stood between him and the woman.

"He gets that a lot," she said. "And who are you?"

The woman frowned. "My bad. I didn't know y'all were together."

"You do now," Kadisha said.

The woman gave Antwon a side eye. "You need to check your woman."

The woman walked away. Antwon did his best to keep from laughing. Kadisha was not amused. They reached the ADOT entrance, passing through security without a hitch.

"You sure we're ice?" Antwon asked.

"We have employment records in their system dating back five years," she said.

"But what if no one recognizes us?"

"The system is always right," Kadisha said. "That's what makes my job so easy. This way."

Antwon followed Kadisha through the building. They took the elevator down to the IT department. The entire area was empty.

"Where is everybody?" Antwon asked.

"They were given the day off," Kadisha replied. "Come on, we only have a few minutes."

Kadisha walked up to one of the consoles and began typing.

"What do you need me to do?" Antwon asked.

"Nothing yet. Just keep an eye on the elevator."

Antwon's attention vacillated between the door and Kadisha. After ten minutes she stood then marched to the hardware. She took out a tool kit and Antwon's eyes bucked. He ran over to and grabbed her hand. Kadisha snarled as she jerked her hand free then punched him hard in the chest, knocking wind out of him. Antwon fell on his ass, gasping.

"Don't touch me!" she spat. "Don't ever touch me!"

Antwon rubbed his chest. "You're installing hardware. Can't do that."

"I have to if you want your plan to work," Kadisha said. "Do you?"

Antwon stood on shaky legs. "Of course, I do."

"Then make up your mind. I put this in and you're a go. I don't, you're fleeked."

Antwon chewed his nails. Hardware was traceable. There was no way he would be able to retrieve it, which meant he was certain to go to jail after Carnival. Was it really worth it?

Antwon lowered his hand.

"Do it," he said.

Kadisha smirked then went to work, opening the console with her tools and installing the chip.

"Let's go," she said.

They took the elevator to the main floor then fast-walked to the exit.

"Hey!"

Antwon and Kadisha turned to see a tall muscular man wearing the maroon blazer and grey slacks of ADOT security, his badge on his pocket. He walked to them then folded his thick arms across his broad chest.

"Who are you, and what were you doing in IT?"

Antwon froze; Kadisha extended her hand.

"Caroline Brooks," she said. "This is Tom Clay. We're from DDOT."

The man's eyes narrowed, and he rubbed his chin.

"I don't see you on my schedule," he said.

"We shouldn't be," Kadisha said. "We received a personal invite from John."

"John Chu?" the security agent asked.

"Is there another John?" Kadisha retorted.

Not only is she lying, she's arrogant about it, Antwon thought. *I like her.*

"I need a few minutes to check this all out," the security guard said.

"We don't have a few minutes," Kadisha replied. "We travelled all the way from Mile High for this meeting and nobody's here. A waste of our time."

The guard reached inside his pocket and pulled out a pair of vidspecs. He put them on then tapped the right side.

"That's unusual. There's been a schedule mix up. Everyone is off today."

"Like I said, a waste of our time." Kadisha nodded at Antwon. "Come on, Tom. Let's go."

Kadisha strode toward the door, Antwon running to catch up.

"Wait!" the guard called out. "We're not finished!"

"Yes, we are," Kadisha called back. "Tell John he owes

me."

Kadisha summoned a Rideout before they were out the door. The vehicle landed as they reached the curb; they climbed inside and they were on their way before the security guard reached the door. Kadisha took a deep breath then exhaled. She looked at Antwon, sharing a wide grin.

"That was fun."

"No, it wasn't," Antwon replied. "You get to go home. This guard's going to see my face on Carnival and put two and two together."

"You're already screwed," Kadisha said. "The hardware, remember?"

Antwon fell back on his seat, massaging his forehead.

"Hey. Here."

Antwon turned his head to Kadisha. She was holding his flash drive.

"I created you a new identity. I didn't give it to you earlier because I didn't know which way you were going to go. Everything is on this. You can ghost for a few months, maybe a few years to let things cool down. You're breaking the law but you're not killing anybody. You can download it from a library console. I think they still have a few units that take flash drives."

Antwon took the flash drive.

"Thanks."

"No problem. I don't do this for everybody, but I like you. You got balls."

"So that's what you call it?"

The Rideout landed at the ATL Tube. The door lifted and Kadisha climbed out.

"Good luck, Antwon. If you get a craving for the Outside,

come visit. It's in your profile."

The Rideout door rose and Kadisha climbed out.

"Enjoy Carnival."

Kadisha smiled then strolled away. Antwon watched her walk away.

"You're a bad ass," he said.

His com buzzed as the Rideout door closed. He swiped his forearm and Marissa's face appeared.

"Hey love. You coming to the rehearsal?"

"I'm on my way."

"Excellent. See you soon."

Marissa's face disappeared and Antwon settled into the Rideout.

"King Center," he said.

Antwon arrived at the centre ten minutes later. He worked his way through the throng leaving the centre, his head down so no one would recognize him. When he reached the door, Marissa greeted him with her big smile and a bigger hug. Her dreads were loose, which meant she had plans for him later. The thought eased his tension a bit, but not all the way. His days of freedom were coming to an end.

"Are they ready?" he asked.

"Yep," Marissa replied. "The last dress rehearsal before Carnival. Wait until you see it."

"I've seen it a thousand times."

"Not like this."

Antwon followed Marissa to the dance hall. Kye and Dame stood in the middle of the floor in costume. They both smiled at him.

"Y'all ready for this?" Kye said.

"Of course," Antwon replied.

"Dim lights," Kye said. The dance hall when completely dark. Marissa grabbed Antwon's ass and he almost laughed.

"Cue music," Kye said.

The beat dropped and Kye and Dame holo-costumes burst out with brilliant light. Kye and Dame became fluid syncopated motion and Antwon was overwhelmed. No matter how many times he's seen the routine in simulation, nothing compared to what he saw at that moment. Kye had worked her magic when he wasn't looking, adding accents and steps that took the dance to the next level. When the music switched from soca to genuine Aytee-El hyper-trap, tears came to Antwon's eyes. Kye and Dame worked the hometown groove like they were born to it, and they were. He had to be honest; they could win Carnival without his surprise.

The music ended and the light came on. Kye and Dame panted, sweated and smiled.

"So?" Dame said.

Antwon couldn't answer. He was wiping his eyes.

"Damn!" Marissa said. "You done danced the man speechless!"

Antwon walked to Dame and Kye and wrapped his arms around both.

"That was so ice!" he said. "I never imagined it could look so tight."

"Sims ain't got nothing on the real thing," Kye said. "Now what do you have planned that could possibly add to this?"

"Get dressed," Antwon said. "We're going to my crib. We'll order up food and I'll show you."

Dame and Kye trotted off to the dressing rooms. Marissa came up behind him and wrapped her arms around his waist.

"I thought it was going to be you and me tonight," she

said.

Antwon turned around in her embrace and hugged her back. He grabbed a handful of her dreads, lifted them to his nose and inhaled. Her hair always smelled so good.

"After they're gone it's going to be you and me until Carnival."

"Hope you took your vits," Marissa whispered.

"Hope you took yours," Antwon replied.

The four of them hopped a Rideout to his crib. Marissa took care of the delivery orders. Ten minutes after they settled in the drop drones arrived with their feast; Jamaican, Soul, Low Country and Trinidadian cuisine from the best restaurants in the city. It was too much to eat in one night, but Antwon didn't care. He was splurging for what probably were his last days of freedom.

After eating their fill, they paired up in the den.

"I wasn't going to show you this," Antwon said. "But I decided I should so you wouldn't be shook when it went down."

"Let's see it already!" Kye said.

The lights dimmed and the simulation began. Antwon watched everyone as they watched the sim. Marissa dropped her fork, spilling oxtails on his Persian rug. Kye covered her mouth with her hands, her eyes glistening. Dame bobbed his head with the music as he laughed.

"This is so ice!" he exclaimed. "So ice!"

Kye uncovered her mouth then turned to look at him.

"I'm glad you shared this. No way I could have danced through this."

Marissa pressed against him then whispered in his ear.

"You're going to jail for this, aren't you?"

Antwon kissed her cheek.

"Most likely."

Her hand found its way between his legs.

"Then let's get rid of the dancing duo. I don't want to waste a minute."

Marissa shooed Dame and Kye from the condo as Antwon cleaned up. He didn't get far; Marissa was pulling at his clothes as soon as the door closed. They were naked before they reached the floor, ignoring the simulation that bathed the room in powder blue light.

Antwon and Marissa spent the next four days in erotic bliss, taking a break from each other to eat leftovers or go to the bathroom. As they passed the time, Aytee-El prepared for Carnival. Traffic was rerouted from the designated areas and decorations were set up by workbots. Music broke out spontaneously, and people danced at random. On Carnival day morning Antwon sat up, rubbing his eyes. Marissa lay beside him, her cute snoring making him laugh.

"Don't be laughing at me, bwoi," she said, her eyes still closed.

"Wake up," he said. "It's Carnival."

Marissa grabbed his arm and pulled him down.

"Wake me up."

Antwon pulled away. "Not this morning. This is it."

Marissa sat up and threw the covers aside.

"Okay." She jumped out the bed then trudged to the bathroom like a disappointed child.

Antwon followed her and they showered, made love, then showered again. They emerged into the condo then dressed slowly.

"So, you're going to this," Marissa said.

"Yep," Antwon replied.

"You don't have to," she said. "The show is good enough as it is."

"But it will be so much better with the rest."

Marissa hugged him. "Fuck the show. Let's get Dame and Kye set up then come back here. They'll be alright."

Antwon stopped buttoning his shirt. He stared at Marissa and she stared back, a pleading look in her eyes. Their relationship had always been casual, but at that moment he sensed they were at the verge of something deeper. Was he ready to give up on a show of the lifetime for it?"

"Come on," he said. "First things first."

They called a Rideout to the Center. Dame and Kye were waiting with the rest of the crew. They all turned toward Antwon and clapped as he entered. Twon the Don was in the house.

"Y'all ready to win this shit?" he shouted.

"Yei yeah!" everyone shouted back.

"Then let's do it!"

The drummers emerged from the crowd and played. Everyone stepped and swayed to the beat before following them out of the building. A crowd waited outside, cheering as they came to the street. Carnival was on. Antwon's crew marched to Peachtree Street and joined the parade, dancing its way to Millennial Park. ATLiens packed the sidewalks, some in costumes, others in casual clothes, all enjoying the music and the celebration. The crews reached the Park and circled the performance area three times, dancing to the same beat. After the third round they took their designated places and the competition began.

The other crews were incredible. Word leaked that Antwon

had something spectacular planned and the crews responded. The entire global union was celebrating Carnival, but the net was focused on Aytee-El. Antwon grew more nervous; Marissa held his hand.

"We got this, love," she said.

"Yeah," he replied. "We got this."

It was their turn. The drummers led a procession to the performing platform, which lowered so Dam and Kye could mount it. Antwon went to the mixing station, replacing the mixer for the Trinis. He swiped his program into the console then waited for Dame and Kye to give him the signal. Kye nodded. They were ready.

"Kill the lights, please," Antwon said. His voice reverberated across the field and the crowd shifted nervously in the darkness.

"ATliens and the world, this is Twon the Don!"

The crowd erupted in claps and cheers. Antwon waited for them to settled down, his finger hovering over the start button. Marissa said he didn't have to do it. She said that Dame and Kye were good on their own. But Marissa was wrong. He had to do it. He had to be his best at all costs, even if it meant going to jail for jacking the grid. He pressed the button.

Dame and Kye appeared in an explosion of light, sound and motion. The crowd was captivated in seconds. Antwon slipped away from the board, seeking a vantage point to see what was about to happen next. As he worked his way back, he saw the lines coming to the performance field. By the time he reached the viewing tower the crowd saw them, too. Every Rideout in the city converged on the field, their lights pulsing in time with the music. Most were empty, but a few held riders who were stunned and confused. The vehicles reached the field then split into separate circles forming a globe of strobing lights around Dame and Kye. The dancers' coloured plumage expanded, enveloping the entire globe. Antwon had reached the top of the viewing tower when something happened that caught him off guard. Every light in the Aytee-El began pulsing with the music.

"By the ancestors!" he whispered.

His cell buzzed and he answered it. Kadisha's smug face greeted him.

"Surprise."

"You're a fleeking genius," Antwon said.

"Every screen on the net is watching right now," Kadisha said. "You're beyond viral. Now the bad news. You have ten minutes before the ADOT shuts it down. You got five minutes to get to the Tube and ghost."

"I'm not going," Antwon said.

"Don't be stupid," Kadisha replied. "Get out of town, get settled then send for Marissa."

"How did you know about Marissa?"

"You keep forgetting who I am. I can scramble the APD GPS and give you another two minutes, but you have to go now.":

"How am I going to get to the station with all the Rideouts..."

A Rideout appeared before him and the door opened.

"Thank you for choosing Rideout."

Antwon jumped inside.

"Destination please?"

"Tube Station Central," Antwon said. He looked and Kadisha smiled.

"You're welcome," she said. "It was good working with

you. Good luck with your new life."

His screen went blank.

Antwon looked back as the Rideout took him to Central Station. The entire city... no, the entire world, was watching. He felt a twinge of sadness because he wouldn't be able to celebrate with his crew, but that was the price of greatness... and freedom. The time would come, and he would make the best of it.

The Rideout touched down at the station. Antwon hurried inside. He didn't take any time to think about where to go. He boarded the first Bullet he saw with the doors open. The scanner collected his credits and confirmed his papers and he sat down beside a middle-aged man with a grey beard. He was watching Dame and Kye on his cell.

The doors closed and the Bullet streaked from the station. Antwon watched the screen, trying to hold back tears of happiness. The man looked at him and smiled.

"It's amazing, isn't it?" he said.

"Yes, it is."

"That Twon the Don is a genius. I can't imagine him doing that by himself."

"He didn't. He had help."

The man looked at him puzzled.

"At least that's what I heard," Antwon said.

"Oh," the man replied.

"Where is this Bullet going, by the way?" Antwon asked the man.

"Lasgidi," the man replied. "Are you visiting?"

"Relocating, actually," Antwon replied. "I've never been."

"You'll love it," the man said.

"I hope so," Antwon replied. "I'm going to be there for a

while."

The viewing screen on the Bullet turned on, broadcasting the performance. Others had joined Dame and Kye on the stage. The party was on.

"You did it, Twon," he whispered. "Yes, you did."

Antwon closed his eyes and let the rhythm lull him to sleep.

*

The Mviti Bullet was late. Agitated Naijans glared at their cells, gestured angrily and yelling as they looked into the dark tunnel for signs of the bullet's arrival. Ten minutes later lights appeared in the distance and the riders released a crescendo of cheers. The bullet from the East African coastal city eased to a stop and crowd monitors rolled into position, clearing a space between the Bullet doors and the expectant passengers.

"Please be patient as passengers disembark," the monitors sang in their generic voice. "Thank you for your cooperation."

The bullet doors slipped open, releasing its passengers. The Naijans foul mood disappeared as they welcomed the arrivals, some returning home, others visiting for the first time. The last person to exit the train was neither. He was a man moving between worlds, at least for the time being.

Antwon was glad to be back in Lasgidi. Although he still didn't consider it home after living there for ten months, it was the most familiar of his haunts. Kadisha warned him not to get too settled and he took her advice to heart. He bounced around the globe, taking low-key deejay jobs and contract sound engineering projects along the way. All the while he kept up with the happenings in Aytee-El. People were still buzzing about Carnival. The ADOT was grilled on how someone could hack their system so completely and the officials had no explanation. Although they knew Antwon was involved, they surmised that he did not have the expertise to pull off such a serious breach. He had help, they said. They were right.

Antwon summoned an okada for the ride home. He called up the heavens and check his accounts as the EV merged into the go-slow.

"Fleek," he said as he looked at his viral account. It was up to 33M cryptos and he couldn't touch it. Carnival feed was making him a wealthy man, but as soon as he touched it APD would be on his ass. He was taking a chance by even looking at it. He shut the link down. His screen took longer than normal to fade; Antwon sat straight when a word scripted in neon flashed in his face.

"Surprise!"

"What the fleek?"

He reached his flat ten minutes later. The word made him nervous. Maybe he spent too much time looking at his account and the APD were on the bullet now. Or maybe it was a joke some hacker was playing on him. Antwon couldn't take any chances. He would have to move.

He entered his flat and was met with the smell of rice and peas, cabbage and oxtails.

"Hey bwoi."

Marissa stood before his stove, wearing a Naija t-shirt and blue jean shorts, her dreads loose. Antwon dropped his bag and ran to her. They kissed for what seemed like hours.

"How did you find me?" he asked.

"Kadisha is a good friend to you," Marissa replied. "She told me where you were two months ago. I wanted to come then but she made me wait. She said she had to fix things."

"Fix things?"

Marissa led him to his couch. Antwon sat down; Marissa sat on his lap.

"She felt bad about what happened to you."

Antwon kissed Marissa's chin. "It wasn't her fault. It was my idea. I got what I deserved. Besides, I feel bad for doing it. You told me I didn't have to."

"And I'm still pissed about that!" Marissa said in mock anger. She popped his head with her hand. "Anyway, she skimmed your virtual funds and hired a law firm to represent you. They're close to coming to a deal with ADOT. She said you should be able to come home in a few weeks."

Antwon frowned. "What's it going to cost?"

"Your virtual account. Every crypto."

Antwon chuckled. "Well, it was nice while it lasted."

He squeezed Marissa. "Doesn't matter. I have all I need right here."

Marissa put her lips near his ear. "We have a few weeks. I hope you took your vits."

Antwon kissed her earlobe.

"I hope you took yours."

Down South
Milton Davis

Roscoe removed his chauffer's hat as he entered Miss Liza's mansion, patting his hair in place with his free hand. Although he worked for Miss Liza for almost 10 years he'd never set foot inside the expansive home on East 127th Street. Whatever she summoned him for must be special.

The maid led him through the antique laden foyer then through the gauntlet of oil portraits hanging on the hallway walls on the way to the parlour. Miss Liza sat before the picture mirror, her ecru skin radiated by the sunlight reflected from the window opposite the mirror. She took a sip of tea then placed the gold inlaid teacup on the matching saucer on the table before her.

"That will be all Celia," she said.

"I'll be right outside if you need me," Celia said as she cast a distrustful glance at Roscoe.

"There's no need for that," Miss Liza replied. "Roscoe drives me every day. If I can't trust him I can't trust anyone."

Celia glared at Roscoe.

"You behave yourself, boy," she whispered

Roscoe glared back. "Mind your own business, you old bitty."

He smiled as he turned his attention to Miss Liza.

"You asked for me, ma'am?" he said.

"Yes I did, Roscoe. Have a seat."

Roscoe sat in the chair next to the door.

Ceila turned toward him. "How long have you worked for me, Roscoe?"

"Ten years come this May," he said.

Miss Liza laughed. "You've outlasted all my husbands."

Roscoe lowered his head, hiding his grin.

"I reckon so, ma'am."

"Aren't you from down South?"

"Yes ma'am."

"Where?" she asked.

"Alabama, ma'am. A little place called Seale."

"I've never heard of it," she said. "My parents are from the South, Atlanta to be exact. But you know that."

"Yes I do, ma'am."

"You fought in the war too, didn't you Roscoe?"

Roscoe tensed. "Yes I did, ma'am. I was a Hellfighter."

Miss Liza knew about his time in the army. He fought in Verdun and earned a medal from the French. He came home thinking that medal and his time served would make a difference, but it didn't. The Klan almost lynched him outside of Phenix City, so he got out the South as soon as he could. If he'd had the money he would have gone back to France. Instead he ended up a taxi driver in New York, where he met Miss Liza. She was so impressed by his manners she hired him as her personal chauffeur.

"Miss Liza, excuse me for being direct, but why did you ask me here?"

Miss Liza's smile faded. "Roscoe, I need you to pick up a

package for me, a very special package."

"That ain't no problem ma'am," he said, somewhat relieved. "Where do I need to go? Brooklyn? Manhattan?"

Miss Liza looked at him square in the eyes. "Savannah, Georgia."

Roscoe shook his head. "I don't think…"

"Listen to me, Roscoe," she said. "You're the only person I can trust to do this. You're from the South so you know how to behave down there. If I sent one of my New York men they'd be lynched before sunset. You're an ex-soldier so you can handle yourself. I'll pay you one thousand dollars up front and one thousand dollars when you return with the package plus all your expenses."

Two thousand dollars would set Roscoe straight for quite some time. But he knew his answer long before Miss Liza began her persuading talk.

"I'm sorry, Miss Liza," Roscoe said. "I can't do it."

"Roscoe please," Miss Liza said. "This is very important to me."

Roscoe put on his hat. "The last thing I want to do is disappoint you ma'am. You've been good to me. But this is one thing I can't do."

"Roscoe…" Miss Liza said.

Roscoe backed out the room.

"I'm sorry, ma'am. I'm sorry."

Roscoe turned then walked away,

"Roscoe, wait!"

Roscoe kept walking. Celia waited at the door, a grin on her face.

"You done messed up now, boy," she said. "Ain't no way Miss Liza going to keep you on now. Good riddance to bad rubbish, I say."

Roscoe pushed by the old maid then continued on to the garage. He trudged up the stairs to his room. Celia was right. He would have to leave and find another job. He was fond of Miss Liza; she reminded him of the daughter he never had. But there were some things he just couldn't do. Going back down South was one of them.

He opened his closet then dragged out his trunk, the same trunk he was issued when he enlisted. He opened it and was engulfed in memories. He gazed upon his uniform, neatly folded and pressed, the Cross de Guerre still pinned to the pocket. Atop the uniform was his bolo knife sheathed in the army issue canvas sheath. He picked up the knife then pulled it free, studying the long, razor edged blade. The last time he held it in his hand was in Phenix City, Alabama. It was the only thing that stood between him and a lynch mob. He closed his eyes then shook the memories from his head. A man who fought for his country shouldn't be treated that way. He had the right to defend himself.

He sheathed the knife then placed it back into the trunk. Roscoe shuffled over to his dresser, opened the drawers then began removing his clothes and placing them neatly into the trunk.

"And where do you think you're going?"

Roscoe turned to see Miss Liza standing in his doorway.

"Well Miss Liza, I figured since I turned down your request you'd be ready to fire me."

Miss Liza sat in his desk chair. "You figured wrong. You're like family, Roscoe, and Lord knows I don't have much of that."

Roscoe sat on the foot of his bed. "I appreciate you think

of me that way. But I don't…"

Miss Liza grabbed his hand.

"Listen to me, Roscoe. I'm going to tell you the whole story. After I'm done if you tell me you won't do it I'll never bother you again."

"I'm listening," Roscoe answered.

Miss Liza swallowed. "When I was 15, I got pregnant. The father was a white boy, Leonard Shuman."

Roscoe leaned back stunned, almost pulling Miss Liza from her seat.

"Pregnant? By a white boy?" Roscoe felt anger rising inside. His grip on Miss Liza's hand tightened.

"It's not what you think, Roscoe," Miss Liza said quickly. "Leonard and I loved each other. Leonard's parents were prominent in New York politics, just like my parents. But Leonard's parents weren't about to let their son marry a coloured girl and my parents weren't about to let me throw my life away on some weak-minded white boy. We fought them but in the end our parents won. Leonard's parents sent him to Europe; my parents sent me to Atlanta where I lived until I gave birth. They took my baby from me then put her up for adoption."

Miss Liza's eyes glistened. Roscoe took a handkerchief from his drawer then handed it to her.

"I held her in my arms, Roscoe. She was so beautiful. I made a promise that day that I would find her, no matter where they took her. Five years ago I did."

"In Savannah?" Roscoe asked. Miss Liza nodded.

"It took a long time and a lot of money but I found her living with foster parents. I sent them a letter explaining who I was and what I wanted to do. I promised I would not try to take her from them. I only wanted to communicate with her. They agreed."

"So you ready to break your promise now," Roscoe said.

"About three months ago my letters started coming back. I've been going crazy ever since. I think she's still in Savannah but for some reason her family decided to stop the letters."

Miss Liza opened her purse, reached inside then took out a picture. She handed the picture to Roscoe.

"Her name is Mary Ann," Miss Liza said.

"She looks just like you," Roscoe said.

"I want my baby, Roscoe. I want my baby home. I'll pay you whatever you want. Please do this for me. Please."

Miss Liza bent over then cried into her hands. Roscoe leaned toward her, placing a gentle hand on her shoulder.

"I'll do it," he said. "I'll go get your baby, Miss Liza."

Miss Liza lunged toward him, wrapping her arms around them.

"Thank you, Roscoe. Thank you!"

Roscoe held her, stroking her hair. He imagined if things had been different for him his own daughter asking him the same question. There would be no doubt he would do it, even if it meant returning to the South and risking his life again.

"It'll be alright, Miss Liza. It'll be alright," he said.

*

The train eased into the Savannah station in the afternoon in the midst of a hot humid day. Roscoe peered out the window, his stomach churning with emotions. During the journey down he'd spent his time lending a hand to the porters, chatting with the black men who served the passengers and kept the train running smoothly. Most were from the South like him, fleeing Jim Crow or seeking a better life in the North. From the chat, nothing much had changed. One conversation with the men warned him to keep on his guard, even though the men didn't realize the warning in their words. They were playing Spades when it began.

Moses Jones, a tall light-skinned man with slick-backed hair dropped a seven of diamonds on the table.

"You fight in the war?" he asked Roscoe.

Roscoe nodded.

"Yeah. I was there, but I wouldn't call it fighting," he lied.

Mike Stevens, a thick muscled man with skin like onyx and glittering white teeth, flashed an easy smile as he cut Moses' seven with a three of spades.

"I think I dug more holes in France than I did in Arkansas," he said.

'Pepper' Lewis, another light-skinned man with freckled cheeks, cursed as he dropped a two of hearts.

"Them boys from the 369th gave them hell, though," he said. "A few of them won medals from the French. You meet any of them, Roscoe?"

Roscoe dropped an eight of spades and everyone moaned.

"No," he said. "I heard they were something else."

"Sho' were," Mike said. "Gave them Huns hell."

"Shoulda stayed in France," Pepper said. "You heard about that one that got lynched in Alabama?"

Everyone but Roscoe shook their heads. Roscoe picked up the cards and shuffled them.

"Say he was coming home and a bunch of Klansmen met him getting off the train in Phenix City, Alabama. Dragged him back in the woods and lynched him."

"That's a damn shame," Moses said. "A goddamn shame."

"You ain't heard the rest of it, though," Pepper said. "Story is every last one of them Klansmen showed up dead. Every last one of them."

Mike folded his arm across his chest. "You a damn liar."

"Kiss my ass, Mike," Pepper said. "I ain't never lied. Some say it was that soldierboy's ghost."

Roscoe quit shuffling the cards, the memory of that night paralyzing him.

"Hey boy, you gonna shuffle them cards?" Pepper said.

Roscoe placed the deck on the table.

"Got to go," he said. "This is my stop."

Pepper laughed. "That story scared you, didn't it?"

Roscoe peered over his shoulder. "Something like that."

Roscoe went back to his seat and gathered his things. The porters had been good company on the way down but it was time to get serious. He waited until he was off the train before opening the leather pouch Miss Liza gave him before the trip. Inside was the address of her daughter's last known residence and a map with directions. Roscoe ventured into the old city, falling into old habits drummed into him since he was a boy. He kept his head down, making sure not to make eye contact with any white folks, especially white women. He was a man of average height, so physically he didn't draw any attention. He deliberately wore his clothes two sizes too big. Most people saw him as overweight; in truth Roscoe was nearly three hundred pounds of hard muscle on a 5'8 inch frame.

He hesitated as he came within a few blocks of his destination. This was a neighbourhood for rich folks. There was no way he would enter without being noticed. What would a coloured girl be doing in this kind of neighbourhood, he thought. He shrugged, Miss Liza was light-skinned, and with her daughter being half white she could probably pass. Roscoe checked the directions one last time.

"Yeah, this is it," he said. "Lord help me."

He proceeded down the manicured street until he reached the address. He was walking up the walkway when the voice startled him.

"Hey boy! Where the hell you think you're going?"

Roscoe turned around to see the policeman standing on the sidewalk, his billy club in his hand. He was a lanky white man with straw blonde hair and a snarl.

"I'm sorry sir, but I was told the people living here were looking for a gardener," Roscoe said.

"They might be, but you know damn well you ain't suppose to be on this walkway. Git on around back!"

Roscoe silently cursed himself. He shuffled down the walkway toward the officer.

"You better be glad I'm in a good mood today, boy," the officer said. "Otherwise I'd take you downtown."

"Much obliged to you, sir," Roscoe said.

"Git on now before I change my mind," the officer said.

"Yes, sir," Roscoe replied. "Yes, sir."

Roscoe walked across the grass then worked his way up the side of the house to the rear entrance, all the while clenching and unclenching his fists. By the time he reached the back of the home he was trembling.

"What you doing back here?" a husky female voice asked.

Roscoe looked up to see a dark brown woman dressed in a sky blue maid uniform hanging clothes on the wire clothes line.

"I came back here to wait on the owners," he said. "I'm

looking for yard work."

"Well you a day late and a dollar short," the woman said.

Roscoe stood then ambled to the fence.

"What do you mean by that?"

"The Finches moved out two weeks ago," she said. "Flew out of here like they owed somebody money. But that ain't so because they got old money."

"My name is Roscoe Hill," Roscoe said.

"Lucinda Jones," the woman said. "Nice to meet you. Where you from?"

"New York," Roscoe said.

Lucinda laughed. "If you from New York then I'm the Queen of England. You sound like you from right around here. Why you trying to be uppity?"

Roscoe laughed. "I'm originally from Alabama."

Lucinda smirked. "I thought so."

Lucinda walked back to the clothesline and began hanging the wash.

"Were they expecting you?"

"Apparently so," Roscoe whispered.

"What?"

"I said I guess not. My boss man said they'd be here."

"Looks like your boss man was wrong," Lucinda said.

"You got any idea where they went?" Roscoe asked.

"I don't, but Mr. Henderson might. He's who I work for. You got a place to stay?"

Roscoe pushed back his hat. "No."

"There's a place called Lulabelle's down by the marsh," Lucinda said. "It's a juke joint, but she has a couple of rooms upstairs she rents out. It's loud but the food is great and it's far enough out of town so no white folks will bother you.

Now come over here and help me hang up these clothes. The sooner I'm done the sooner I can leave."

"Your boss won't mind?"

"Hell naw," Lucinda said. "As long as he ain't got to pay you he's fine. He'll probably think you some old buck sweet on me."

Roscoe grinned as he made his way next door. Lucinda wasn't a bad looking woman, but she was way too young for him. Besides, he was in Savannah on business. He helped her hang the rest of the laundry then went out front to wait for her. She came from around back, a wide smile on her face.

"Give me your arm," she said.

Roscoe extended his arm and Lucinda wrapped hers around it.

"Now we're sweethearts until Mrs. Henderson can't see us no more."

Roscoe glanced at the house. The curtain was pulled aside; a white woman with a blonde bun on top of her head glared at them.

They strolled down the road until they were far from the house and into the city. Lucinda let go of Roscoe. The two strolled to Black Savannah, a section of town that was in complete contrast to the newer section north and South of the city. Though the boll weevil destroyed the cotton crops, Savannah still thrived on shipping naval stores. The city had grown because of the prosperity, but like most cities that prosperity barely touched Negroes.

Lucinda walked up to a grocery store then began walking inside.

"I thought we were going to Lulabelle's," Roscoe said.

"We are. I got to pick up a few things before I go home."

"I need to get something too," Roscoe said.

They entered the grocery store. Lucinda strolled about the little store picking up items here and there; Roscoe went straight to the tool barrel. He searched through the tools until he found a sturdy long handled shovel. When he met Lucinda at the counter her eyes went wide.

"Now what in the devil's name do you need that for?"

"I'm a yard man," Roscoe said. "It always helps to have a good shovel."

Roscoe and Lucinda strolled down the street until they reached the edge of the coloured district.

"This is as far as I go," Lucinda said. "Keep walking that way. You'll smell the marsh before you see it. Once you get inside ask for Slow Tom. He owns the place."

"Slow Tom?"

Lucinda laughed. "We call him that because he's the smartest man in Savannah."

"Thank you, Lucinda."

"You'll thank me by buying me dinner once you finish your business."

Roscoe looked puzzled. "My business?"

Lucinda tilted her head. "You might fool them white folks, but you ain't fooled me. I know you ain't no yard man. I don't know what business you got with the Finches and I don't want to know. All I can say is be careful. This ain't New York."

"I'll be getting on then," Roscoe said.

By the time Roscoe reached the marsh the moon had risen over the humid night. The light wavered on the high tide, the air heavy with the wetland organic aroma. The sound of raucous laughter spurred on by a teasing melody of guitar and piano drifted toward him as he neared Lulabelle's. The large barn-like structure sat on a piece of land jutting into the marsh, surrounded by ancient live oaks heavy with Spanish moss. A tall man in coveralls leaned against a pickup truck, cradling a double-barreled shotgun in his thick arms. The man stood up straight as Roscoe approached.

"Who is that?" the man said in a thin, high pitched voice.

Roscoe walked into the light with his hands raised.

"Roscoe Jones," he said. "Miss Lucinda told me I could find a place to stay the night here."

The man motioned Roscoe forward with the shotgun.

"Where you from?" he asked.

"Alabama, by way of New York."

The man smiled. "I'm Percy Green. My niece Corliss lives in New York. You know a girl named Corliss Lewis?"

"Can't say I do. New York is a big place."

"Yeah but all the coloured folks live in Harlem," the man said. "You sure you don't know her? Tall, yellow gal with big teeth."

"No, I don't know her."

The doorman shrugged. "Go on in. Slow Tom will be behind the bar. Can't miss him."

Roscoe nodded then went inside. The blues band was playing a slow, heavy tune, the dancers slow dragging to the beat, grasping and grinding. Roscoe made his way across the packed floor toward a wide man with a bald head, a cigar protruding from the side of his mouth. His thick hands worked on a large beer mug as he rocked to the music.

"You Slow Tom?" Roscoe asked.

Slow Tom looked at Roscoe and his eyes narrowed.

"Who's asking?"

"Roscoe Tillman," Roscoe said. "Miss Lucinda told me

you rent rooms to coloured folks."

Slow Tom placed the mug on the bar then extended his right hand. They shook, Slow Tom attempting to crush Roscoe's hand with his grip. He yelped when Roscoe returned the favour. When he finally let go Tom jerked his hand away as if he'd touched fire.

"Damn, boy! Where's you get a grip like that?"

"Grew up on a farm," Roscoe replied. It was half the truth.

"Rooms are a dollar a night. Might as well stay up until I close. Won't get much sleep with this going on. You play cards?"

"No, sir," Roscoe replied.

"Quit with that sir stuff. Just call me Tom."

Roscoe reached into his pocket then handed Tom a dollar.

"Now that's the kind of boarder I like!" Tom said. "Man pays up front. You hungry?"

"Yes I am," Roscoe replied.

"I'll fix you up. Sit on down and I'll have Hatty mix you up a bucket."

Slow Tom turn then pushed the swing door behind him open.

"Hey Hatty! Fix up a bucket! I got paying folks out here!"

Roscoe took a seat at the bar just as the music tempo picked up. Some of the couples reluctantly let go of each other, others took their business outside. Tom dropped a mason jar in front of Roscoe and grinned.

"Good stuff," he said. "Made it myself."

Roscoe picked up the jar then took a swing. It was good moonshine, stronger and smoother than most. He would need some liquid encouragement for what he was about to do.

"Good stuff," Roscoe said. "How much?"

"First one is on the house," Tom said.

Roscoe finished the glass then wiped his mouth with his sleeve.

"Hey Tom, you know anything about a white family called Finch?"

"I don't," Tom said. "But their maid Corliss does. She came in here mad as hellfire. Said the Finches let her go without even a warning. Said they were moving."

"When did that happen?"

"About three weeks ago. She said they got a letter then lost their minds. Rumour is they went to hide out in the marsh."

So the Finches had been warned about his coming, Roscoe surmised. And he knew exactly who warned them.

"Any idea where that house is?" Roscoe asked.

The kitchen door swung wide and Hatty came out with a steaming bucket, a wash towel wrapped around the metal wire handle. She dropped the bucket between Tom and Roscoe. Her eyes lingered on Roscoe as a grin came to her face.

"You gonna have to teach that boy how to eat crabs," she said. "He ain't from around here."

Tom took a crab out the bucket then instructed Roscoe the proper way to crack a crab.

"Why you trying to find them white folks so bad?" Tom asked.

"I have a special delivery for them," he said. "My boss man told me to deliver it directly to them, nobody else."

"He picked a coloured man for the job?"

"My boss man is coloured."

Tom sucked the meat out of a crab leg.

"They're hiding out at the old Wallace Plantation about five miles from here. But you better have business with them.

They got some local rednecks standing guard. You might mess around and get lynched."

"I'll be alright," Roscoe said. "That's been tried before. Didn't work out too well for them."

Tom began to laugh until he saw Roscoe's serious face.

"Do me a favour; when you get caught, don't mention my name. I got to live here."

Roscoe was working on his third crab.

"I won't."

The men finished their meal as the band slowed down the music again for another round of slow dragging. Roscoe laid two dollars on the counter for the meal but Tom waved him off.

"You don't make a man pay for his last meal," he said.

Roscoe took the bills.

"You think your man can take me close?"

Tom laughed. "You give Percy five dollars and he'll take you to the moon."

"Much obliged," Roscoe said.

He tipped his hat then went outside. Percy leaned against the pick up truck, whistling.

"Hey Percy, Slow Tom says you'll take me anywhere I want to go for five dollars."

"Hell yeah!" Percy replied.

Roscoe handed Percy the five dollar bill.

"I'll give you another five if you'll wait for me," Roscoe said.

"It's a deal. Where we going?"

"Spanish Wells," Roscoe said.

Percy hopped into the truck and they drove deeper into the marsh. After a few more miles Percy stopped the truck.

"This is as far as I go," he said.

Roscoe climbed out the truck then took his shovel from the bed.

"I'll be back," he said.

He trotted down the narrow road through a gauntlet of live oaks. A few minutes later a large house came into view. Roscoe counted six men in the front, four standing guard near the gate and two on the porch with rifles or shotguns. Roscoe slowed to a saunter as he walked into view.

"Who's there?" one of the men shouted. Roscoe didn't answer.

"God damn it, who is it?" the man said again.

Two of the guards approached him, their guns still cradled under their arms.

"Boy, what the hell are you doing out here this time..."

Roscoe smashed the man in the face with the shovel. He knocked the gun from the other guard's hand then reached behind his back for the knife. As soon as his hand touched the hilt he was back in Seale, Alabama, surrounded by the sights and sounds of that horrible night. He cut the guard across his throat then sprinted for the house.

He heard a rifle report then flinched as a bullet struck his shoulder. He gritted his teeth and his body expelled the bullet then commenced healing. Other men appeared from behind the house. Roscoe counted twenty in all. He had worse odds in France. He waited until they were all close before he went to work. Roscoe stabbed, cut and slashed his way through the bodyguards, every blow a killing blow. Thirteen bodies lay sprawled on the ground before the others realized this was no ordinary man they were dealing with. They tried to run, but Roscoe caught them then dragged them back to his blade. He managed to glance toward the house; he saw a car pull from the back then speed up the narrow road. He looked about; five men were still alive, each running in a different direction. If he wanted to get Miss Liza's daughter he would have to let them go.

He wiped his knife then tucked it in the back of his pants. Roscoe started with a slow gait then picked up the pace with each step. He ran down the dirt road then onto the paved street, increasing his speed. Soon the rear lights of a car came into view. He assumed by how fast it travelled, it was the car he sought. Roscoe ran faster; in a few moments he was side by side with the car, peering into the passenger's side. A young woman sat there; she looked up, saw him then screamed. The driver swerved then looked at him as well. Roscoe lowered his shoulder then rammed it into the car. The driver lost control then spun across the road and into the surrounding marsh. Roscoe hurried to the car. The driver leaned over the steering wheel rubbing his head. The girl looked at him as if he was death. He reached for the door but the girl locked it. Roscoe gripped the door handle then ripped the door free.

"Don't be afraid," Roscoe said. "Your mama sent me."

The man in the driver's seat pulled out a gun. Roscoe snatched the woman from her seat then turned his back as the man fired. The bullets struck him hard and he fell forward. He caught himself, hovering the young woman. He heard the man grunt as he exited the car.

"Get up and turn around," the man ordered.

Roscoe sprang up, knocking the gun from the man's hand. He wrapped his hand around the man's throat then lifted him off his feet.

"Now you listen to me Leonard, and you listen good,"

Roscoe said. "I'm taking Mary Ann to her mother where she belongs. Y'all could have worked things out, but I guess it's way beyond that now."

"I'm her father!" Leonard said.

"You done took everything from Miss Liza. You ain't going to take her daughter, too. Now I'm going to put you down and you're going to get in that car and keep driving until you get back to where you came from. And you ain't never going tell anybody what happened here. If you do, I'll find out. And the next time I won't be so nice."

Roscoe set the man down on his feet. He glanced at the woman then scrambled to the car, started the engine then sped into the darkness. When Roscoe turned to the woman, she cowered.

"Don't hurt me!" she said.

Roscoe reached into his jacket then took out the letter Miss Liza sent with him.

"This is from your mama," he said.

Mary Ann reached out with a trembling hand then took the letter. She opened it; as he read it her fear gave way to joy. She folded the letter.

"So you're Roscoe," she said. "Mama told me a lot about you, but I guess not everything."

Roscoe nodded. "You can't tell what you don't know. I'm trusting that you can keep a secret."

"I can," the woman said.

"Good. Now let's get you to New York."

Roscoe picked up the woman.

"Hold on tight," he said.

Mary Ann held his neck tight and Roscoe sprinted down the road back to Percy's truck. The man was snoring."

"Percy!"

Percy jumped his eyes wide.

"Where? What?"

He looked at Roscoe and the woman and eyes got bigger."

"Where the hell you get that white woman from?"

"I'm not white," Mary Ann said.

Roscoe walked over to the passenger's side then put the woman into the truck.

"You'll be alright now," he said.

"Thank you, Roscoe," she said.

Roscoe nodded then walked back to the passenger side. He gave Percy ten dollars.

"Percy this is Miss Mary Ann Pritchard. You take this woman to the train station and stay with her until she boards," Roscoe said.

"Where you going?"

"I got some cleaning up to do."

"Got it."

Percy sped off down the road. The woman looked back at him with a warm smile.

Roscoe set himself then returned to the Wallace plantation. He found his shovel then proceeded to dig a deep hole. Then he piled all the dead men into the hole and covered it the best he could. The sun was breaking the eastern horizon as he finished. This was a sloppy job, but he didn't have time to make it right. Word would spread soon on what happened at Wallace Plantation and he would need to be long gone by then. He heaved the shovel far into the marsh, then ran into the forest shadows.

*

Franklin Stevens took off the blood-stained apron then washed his hands. Working at the slaughterhouse wasn't the best job he's ever had but it definitely wasn't the worst. He was working, which during these times was a blessing. He trudged to his locker, taking out his coat, hat and scarf. Chicago winters were brutal, and this winter was no exception. Despite the cold he walked back to his flat, relishing the quiet time. Sometimes a man just needed to be alone with his thoughts.

His landlord stood in the lobby as he entered the building. He had a sly smile on his face that bothered Franklin.

"Rent due?" he asked.

"No," the landlord replied.

"So why you looking at me?"

The landlord grinned. "You'll see."

Franklin shook his head then climbed the stairs to the third floor. He opened his door then stepped inside. He took off his coat and scarf, hanging them on the coat stand near the door.

"Roscoe?"

He stiffened at the sound of an old name from a familiar voice.

He turned around to see Miss Liza sitting at his table.

"Miss Liza," he said.

"It took me a long time and a lot of money to find you," she said.

Roscoe took off his hat. Miss Liza stood then rushed him, wrapping him in a tight hug.

"Thank you so much for sending my baby back to me!"

Roscoe held Miss Liza for a moment then let her go. He walked over to the door then opened it.

"You're welcome. Now I think you best be leaving."

Miss Liza seemed startled.

"Leaving? I just found you! I have so much to tell you, so many questions to ask…"

"I can't answer your questions and there's nothing I need to hear," he said. "I know the both of y'all is alright. You know I'm alright. That's got to be enough."

"Roscoe, please."

Roscoe shook his head.

"I'm suspecting Mary Ann told you everything."

Miss Liza's face became serious. "Yes."

"The more you know about me, the less safe you are. There are people out there looking for me and I'm trying my best not to be found. You understand?"

Miss Liza nodded. "I found you."

"Which is why I'm going to leave this place."

Miss Liza gathered her things then walked to the door. She placed her hand on Roscoe's cheek then kissed him.

"You take care of yourself, Roscoe. If you ever get tired of hiding, you have a home with me and Mary Ann."

Roscoe closed his eyes hard to cut off the tears he knew were coming.

"Goodbye Miss Liza."

Miss Liza's hand lingered on his check a moment longer before she left his flat. He closed the door then sat hard at his table. He gave himself a moment, letting a few tears fall before wiping his face. He went to his closet then opened his trunk, gazing at the old uniform and the knife.

"One day," he whispered. "One day."

He took his clothes off the hangers and began to pack.

The Swarm
Milton Davis

Famara Keita shielded his eyes from the bright dry season sun, his shesh protecting his face from the stinging, windblown sand. His Sokoto stallion stirred restlessly, agitated by the scene before them. A wide stretch of barren land stretched to the horizon. It was a scene that would be normal in the Sahara, but this was the Sahel, a region that even in its driest was covered by grass and clumps of shrubs.

"By the ancestors," he said.

He nudged his horse into the emptiness. Dust whorls rose before the horse's hooves as Famara scanned the waste for some indication of life in the expanse. Though he had no clue what had occurred, it was obvious the Elders were right to send him to this place.

He was thankful for his provisions, for there was nothing as far as he could see. His horse was another matter. With no grass to graze they were forced to continue through the desolation until they found where the devastation ended. It took most of the day to the edge of night before they found the end of the barrens. The horse picked up its pace instinctively. Soon they were among the grasses, a lake shimmering in the distance.

Famara reached into his bag for his binoculars; he spotted a village on the far side of the lake, fishing boats bobbing on the murky water. He would travel to the village in a few days, hoping to find someone that could describe to him what had occurred. For the moment he would set up camp then analyse the remains for clues.

He dismounted then unpacked his horse, allowing it to wander into the grasses. It took him a long while to set up camp. He travelled heavier than normal, but the extra gear was necessary. After setting up camp he walked to the lake. The water was fairly pure, good enough for drinking and perfect for his steam generator. He carried the water back to camp in the leather folding bucket he'd brought with him. It took him a moment to set up the table that would serve as lab bench. Once the equipment was set up, he filled the steam generator with coal and water, igniting the coal with flint and grass. The generator emitted a rhythmic chugging sound; soon the table was illuminated by the soft light of his portable lamps. He lit a citronella oil lamp, driving away the insects drawn by the faint light, then walked into the sand to gather sample. Hunger interrupted his duties.

After a quick meal of sorghum, he set up his makeshift lab. He sat the microscope close to the lanterns then removed the dirt samples he'd collected earlier. Famara was a horro, a warrior for the Elders, but the ndoki trained him to run simple tests when such knowledge was required. They supplied him with different solutions which, when in contact with the proper chemicals, would change colour to indicate the presence of certain materials. He sprinkled the debris on a glass slide then placed it under the microscope. The granules enlarged under the lenses, revealing a multicoloured array of particles. This was not just sand, to Famara's displeasure. He took the first indicator solution, squeezing a drop onto the slide. The sand turned a dark green. Famara frowned; the indicator revealed pieces of human flesh among the particles. The amount present dismissed the possibility of the flesh being random. The indicator confirmed the rest of the rumour. The locusts were devouring everything, people included.

He gathered then tested more samples to confirm his findings. After the tenth sample there was no doubt with what he found. The locusts were consuming everything. He pushed back from his table, his brow furrowed in disbelief. How could these insects change their habits so drastically?

He looked toward the village on the lake again. If there were any answers, he would find them there. He unpacked his cot, then built a small fire and brewed a pot of tea. The drink relaxed him; after a few more sips he succumbed to his fatigue and slept.

Famara woke to screams. He sat upright, throwing his blanket aside then gathering his weapons. After mounting his horse, he looked in the direction from which the cries came. The village was under attack. A black cloud swirled over and through it, the people running and flailing against the unnatural onslaught. They scattered in every direction attempting to escape. When a person fell the darkness condensed around them, diminishing them into nothingness. A swirling tendril rose from the carnivorous cloud, slowly drifting in Famara's direction. Famara searched about, his eyes finally settling on the lake. It was a good distance away but it was his only chance.

There was no way he could save his horse. He jumped off the beast then slapped its rump hard, sending it galloping in the opposite direction. It had a better chance of avoiding the swarm in the open. With the horse well on its way, Famara sprinted toward the lake, shedding his items along the way. The swarm sped toward him, descending over the lake. He raised his arms, protecting his face as well as he could. If he could only reach the lake…

Locusts pelted his body as he splashed into the lake's edge. His exposed flesh stung from numerous bites, spurring his descent into the murky water. His hands bled as he completely submerged. The swarm crashed against the lake surface like lethal rain, swimming inches under the surface a few inches before falling still. Famara swam deeper, fighting to hold his breath as the swarm hovered over the surface awaiting his ascent. Reaching his limit, he swam to the surface, took a breath then descended again, managing to avoid the vicious bites. On his third ascent the swarm had dispersed. Famara trod water for a moment, then swam to shore. When he looked to the opposite bank he was astonished to see the entire village gone. He looked down; hundreds of locust bodies floated on the lake surface. He scooped up a handful then carried them to where his camp was set up. He put the locusts into his pouch then dug with his hands into the sand until he reached his equipment and provisions. He busied himself with setting up the microscope again, fighting to keep his mind off the horror that just occurred and staying focused on his mission. Once the microscope was ready he took a locust from his pouch then placed it under the lenses.

It was not an insect. It was a miniature clockwork construct, a device designed by a master of diminutive machines, most likely someone with experience in watch making. Famara increased the magnification, studying the locust's antennae. They consisted of thin copper wire, indicating the locusts were probably guided by some frequency radiated from a specific spot nearby. They probably responded to simple commands; if it was a frequency then it could be scrambled. A single passage ran from the locust's mouth to its anus. The creature was designed to work like a steam-powered saw, chewing up anything in its path then discharging it. Whoever controlled the locusts had to be within sight to control the attack, which meant he had been seen.

The artificial insect's wings were powered by a tiny spring. Famara searched for a winding mechanism and found it on the thorax between the wings. He searched his pouch and retrieved a tiny straight wrench, which he clamped over the winding key then turned as delicately as he could. No sooner did he finish winding the locust did the antennae twitch.

"It's receiving a signal," Famara said aloud. He quickly located a length of string, then tied it around the locust's thorax and around his wrist. The locust's wings fluttered and the bug flew from under the microscope lens, its escape halted by the spring.

The locust would lead him to the source, Famara thought. He would wait to see if his horse would return. If not, he would set off on foot. The horse did finally return, close to dusk, too late for him to travel. He decided to set up camp near the lake just in case the locusts returned. The night was a restless one, the locust constantly tugging for freedom while images of the village massacre repeated in his head. He'd served the elders since his manhood rites and had seen many sights, both pleasant and horrible, but never had he seen a village destroyed in such a manner. This was violence for no purpose, something that would only spark terror.

Maybe that was the reason. Someone was using the locust

to frighten the villagers and force them to leave. The Elders had given him three tasks; locate the source of the threat; discover if a Book was involved and if so, obtain it; and determine if the person or persons using the technology of the Book were worth incorporating into their circle. If not, they were to be eliminated. Famara had known the moment he saw the village attacked by the swarm what his decision would be.

*

The workers trudged though the hot sun and ankle-deep sand, their umber skin glistening with sweat. The large stones bending their backs had been carved from the nearby mountains and carried the entire distance. The men staggered to the edge of the thorn bush filled moat then dropped their stones before the masons, who positioned the huge carved rocks along the moat borders, plastering them together with mortar. A thorn bush moat ringed the city's outer perimeter, a single retractable bridge leading to a towering stone gate. Wooden towers were positioned at measured distances, occupied by warriors armed with rifles. Horsemen circled the perimeter every two hours.

Famara lowered his binoculars then placed them at his side. He opened his canteen, taking another swig of water. The wind up locust tugged at his wrist, still following the signal calling it home. Over the three days he'd observed the city he'd seen swarms leave and return from every direction. He imagined the terror and destruction they left behind and anger boiled in his gut. He shuffled backwards until he was out of sight of the towers before standing on his feet and walking to his horse. The city was the origin of the swarm and, most likely, where the Book he sought was kept. Whoever controlled it was preparing for an attack. The defeces would be formidable once completed; Famara would have to make his move soon or entry would be too difficult. He would wait until dusk to implement his plan.

As the sun eased below the western horizon, Famara mounted his horse then rode up the hill, hiding his presence. As he crested the hill he raised his spyglass, studying the fortifications once more. The gate swung open and three riders emerged, galloping in his direction. He watched them for a moment then reined his horse, galloping away as if fleeing. He rode a distance, dismounted his horse then waited. The riders crested the hill and rode up to him, pistols drawn. Famara turned to face them, his hand raised. Two of the men dismounted and strode toward him; the third remained on his horse.

"Who are you?" the lead man said in Arabic.

"Just a traveller," Famara replied.

"A traveller with a spyglass?" the man replied. "I think not."

"I was looking to see if your village was a hospitable place to spend the night," Famara explained. "As I suspected, it is not."

"Kill him and be done with it," the man on the horse said.

Famara twisted out of the line of fire as he reached behind his back, throwing his knife at the mounted rider. The knife struck the man in the face and he fell from his horse. Famara dropped low, spinning with his leg extended. Both men fired their pistols as the horro swept them off their feet. He pounced on them before they could react, slicing one man's throat while clubbing the other on the head. He hurried to the man felled by his throwing knife, making sure he was dead. Famara exchanged clothes with the man, ignoring the tight fit. He dressed the man in his garments then trotted back to the clubbed man, who was regaining consciousness. Famara pulled his arms forward then tied his wrists together with a thin rope. When the man fully revived Famara squatted before him, his pistol in the man's face.

"Up," he said.

The man climbed to his feet. Famara motioned toward the man's horse and the man climbed onto the steed.

"Try to ride away and you'll get a bullet in your back," Famara warned. Famara placed the dead men on their steeds then mounted his horse. He gave the reins of the horse carrying the man in his clothes to his prisoner.

"What is your name?" Famara asked.

"Didinga," the man said.

"Who controls this city, Didinga?" Famara asked.

"Amadou Soros," the man replied.

Famara's eyes widened. "You're lying!"

He struck Didinga and he fell off his horse.

"I speak the truth!" Didinga said.

Famara sat before the man, rubbing his head.

"Amadou? It can't be..." he whispered.

After a moment he stood, lifting the man up.

"Get on."

The man clambered onto the horse and Famara gave him the reins of the dead man's horse once again.

"Ride ahead of me," Famara ordered. "We gallop through without stopping. If anyone asks why, you tell them I'm wounded. Once we're in the stables you will take me to

Amadou. Understand?"

Didinga winched as he nodded.

They galloped up and over the hill, Famara following with the other dead mounted man. As they approached the gate Famara heard the familiar hiss of a steam engine and the doors creaked open. Two guards stood on either side of the entrance, rifles lowered. A third man blocked their entrance.

"Keep going," Famara said.

"But I will…"

"Keep going!" Famara shouted.

The man blocking their way tried to stop them, waving his hands and shouting. At the last minute he jumped out of the way.

Famara and Didinga rode into the stables. Famara jumped off his horse then snatched Didinga off his horse.

"Let's go now!" he said.

The guards approached. The man who attempted to block them came closer.

"Didinga! Jakada! You almost trampled me!"

The man had mistaken Famara for the dead Jakada.

"Jakada is wounded," Didinga said. "I'm taking him to the healer. Fahru and the interloper are dead."

The men changed directions, walking toward the horses. Famara nudged Didinga.

"I'll take care of it," he said. "Get back to your posts."

The men shrugged, then did as they were told.

"Which building?" Famara asked.

"That one," Didinga said, nodding toward a large stone structure in the centre of the village. From a distance it resembled a mosque, but as they drew nearer Famara could see it was designed for industrial pursuits. The structures resembling minarets were actually dormant smokestacks, the entrance wide to accommodate any large contraptions entering or leaving the structure. As they neared the building a familiar buzzing sound reached Famara's ears.

"A swarm," he said.

Didinga flinched when he heard the word.

"I hate those damned things!" he said. "I saw them chew a man to dust."

"I saw them do the same thing to an entire village," Famara said.

Didinga turned to face him, his eyes wide.

"It's those Books!" he said. "They are filled with evil."

"It's not the Books," Famara replied. "It's the man wielding them. Where did you see the Books?"

Didinga pointed to the building. Famara shoved him toward the structure. There were no guards outside; Amadou was apparently comfortable with his security. As they entered the building Famara saw a huge chamber filling the centre of the building. Mechanical locusts swirled inside, their buzzing filling the vacuous chamber.

"His laboratory is behind the chamber," Didinga said. "Come, I'll show you."

They skirted the edge, Famara remaining vigilant. They reached the opposite end of the building, standing before another door.

"Open it," Famara ordered.

Didinga grasped the latch then opened the door.

"Didinga, what are you doing here?" A familiar voice said. "What do you want?"

Famara shoved Didinga into the room then followed.

"I should ask you the same questions," Famara said.

Amadou Soros looked up from his bench, a knowing smile slowly coming to his bearded face. He stood, revealing the body of a former horro, his muscular frame clear through the single tobe he wore. He placed the tools he held on the surface, his hands going to his waist.

"Hello, Famara," he said. "I can't say seeing you here is unexpected. I hoped I would have more time."

"Your time became short when you began murdering people with your bugs," Famara replied. "How could you do this? This is not our way!"

"How could I not?" Amadou replied. "The Elders lied to us, Famara. They have no plans to use the knowledge of the Books to heal the world."

"You're wrong and you know it," Famara said. "You've been to Wagadu. You've seen the wonders there."

"Wonders that benefit no one. How long must the world wait before the Elders bestow their blessings upon us?"

"That is their decision to make," Famara said.

Amadou smiled. "Not any more."

Didinga's foot scraped the floor, warning Famara. He ducked instinctively, avoiding the man's double-hand blow. He twisted, driving his fist into the man's stomach, then rolled to avoid Amadou's throwing knife. Famara rose with pistols in both hands. Amadou dove before he fired and the bullets struck the wall behind him. Amadou pulled his own gun and the men shot as they sought cover. Didinga charged Famara again; the horro knocked him unconscious with a kick to the face. Amadou used the distraction to flee the hangar, taking the Books with him. Famara had no idea where the man fled. There was only one way to find out.

He hurried to the chamber holding the locusts. He took a

throwing knife then lodged it into the seam of the chamber door. He opened the handle, slipping a stick of explosive into it. Famara raised his shesh over his mouth and nose as he walk backwards. Once he thought he was far enough away, he raised his handgun then fired. The knife exploded, blasting the chamber open. Famara was already running as the locusts poured from the chamber. With no signal to guide them, they descended on everything in sight. Didinga was consumed in unconsciousness, the tables and the hangar their next targets. Famara swatted away a few errant locusts as he made way toward the stables. The others were still there examining the bodies on the horses. Famara shot them down before mounting his horse, reining it to full gallop toward the still open gate. Halfway to the exit the locusts burst from the hangar, attacking everything before them. Famara rode through the gate, pushing his mount relentlessly as they crossed the open grasslands. There was no lake for refuge, only the hope the locusts would wind themselves down within the village and not seek out more beyond the unfinished walls.

Two hours later his horse refused to go any farther. Famara jumped from the horse then ran a bit farther before turning to look in the city's direction. No dark cloud swirled behind him. He took out his spyglass. The walls still stood, but the wooden buildings beyond them were gone. Famara looked in every direction but saw no signs of the swarm. Logic told him the mechanical devourers had consumed everything and everyone in the camp and spent themselves, but he had to be sure. He studied the area for another hour before grabbing his horse's reins and walking back toward the city.

It was midday when he reached the outskirts. Famara released the horse then entered the city. The ground was littered with the vile locusts; human remains were scattered about. He entered the hangar to a similar scene, the only remaining object the metal chamber that held the insects. He searched every building, hoping to find some remains of the Books. As he reached the opposite side of the city he realised that would not be. The locusts had done their job.

He was leaving when he noticed something stir to his right. Locusts rose from the sand then flew to each other. Other locusts rose around him then joined the small swarm. Instead of attacking him they flew toward the east.

"Amadou," Famara said.

He ran back to his horse, mounted and galloped through the city. He found camel tracks in the sand, heading the same direction of the fading swarm.

"This is not over," Famara whispered. "But it will be."

He snapped his horse's reins and they galloped together after the swarm.